T0198587

STAKEHOLDER MANAGEMENT

STAKEHOLDER MANAGEMENT

New Words for Old Ideas

Garth Holloway

To order additional copies of this book, contact:
Xlibris
1-800-455-039
www.Xlibris.com.au
Orders@Xlibris.com.au
761657

Acknowledgements

With thanks to: Shamim Ur Rashid for the cover design;

Nidhan Singh for the graphics;

Stephany Aulenback for editing the book;

Charles Goudman and Kailash Krishnan for their support, critique and friendship.

Dedication

To my late mom with all my love. If anybody understood stakeholder management, she did.

Contents

Preface

Thank you for taking the time to read my book.

The book provides insights on how to engage and manage stakeholders through a business transformation program. The principles discussed would be applicable in any situation where stakeholders require management, but the book is particularly focused on business transformation.

Each chapter was originally published as a standalone article. The articles have been brought together as a book in their original form.

There is some overlap between the two chapters on stakeholder communications and messaging (talking to stakeholders). This is due to the close relationship between the two topics.

This book does not deal with the subtler points of change management and business improvement methodology. These concepts are addressed in separate books.

Collectively, there are four books in the series: "Stakeholder Management," "Change Management," "Management Concepts and Models," and "The Manager's Kitbag." They combine to provide a powerful insight into the world of business transformation and change.

Management Accountability

A significant challenge for any large business improvement program is how to enlist the senior stakeholder community into the change program and keep them engaged. Senior stakeholders can be relied on to show an interest in the change program when it starts, but their interest will often fade as "business as usual" issues dominate the day-to-day operations.

Then, as the business improvement program progresses, the change team becomes mired in the detail and withdraws into their own world. They spend their time looking at data, completing risk reviews, agreeing the way forward, mapping processes, and preparing papers that will describe the desired outcome. The longer this goes on, the more introspective the change program becomes and the less the senior stakeholders are engaged by the change program.

The seasoned change agent knows that change is not sustainable without tangible support from senior stakeholders, and that getting the senior managers to change their daily routines, habits, and behaviours is very difficult. And it becomes more impossible the longer their behaviour is left unchallenged. The reason it goes unchallenged is that the change team believes that until they have worked through the detail, they don't have anything meaningful to say, and they don't want to waste the senior managers' time.

The problem is that the senior managers run the company, not the change program. It is important that they stay engaged. But if the change agent is going to engage the senior managers, then they need to be able to frame the conversation and have an agenda.

When it comes to change, there is no better agenda than talking to managers about what they are or aren't accountable for. If you can't get a manager to agree on their own accountability, then you can be sure that the outcomes of the business improvement program will be less than optimal.

There are many models that support a conversation on accountability. The most common is the R.A.C.I. (RACI) model. It is a simple model, but the practical application of this model is beset with problems, the biggest of which is the question of what the acronym actually stands for.

The generally accepted definition is that it refers to: Responsible, Accountable, Contributor (or Consulted), and Informed.

This definition is misleading. The "A" cannot stand for Accountable as all four dimensions have accountability. A manager is accountable for being informed or contributing. It is not the job of the change agent or process performer to inform management. It's management's job to ensure that they are informed. The business holds them accountable to be informed. How can you manage if you are uninformed?

In the same sense, managers are accountable for approving a process outcome. This means they need to know what the outcome should be, what control points they should have considered, and what delegations of authority might apply. If the manager plays an active role in the process, then they are accountable for being responsible for doing their part of the process properly.

In terms of a business improvement program, when the change team approaches a manager designated as a Contributor for comment, that manager is accountable for making time and providing a well-thought-out contribution to the discussion.

Apart from the confusion arising from the fact that all four variables have accountability, there is a second misunderstanding about the RACI model, namely that it only applies within a business process.

Consider the graphic below. When RACI is applied within a process then it can be argued that the Supervisor approves the process outcomes, Role 1 is responsible for Steps 1 and 2, Role 2 contributes to Step 1 and Role 3 is informed by Role 2.

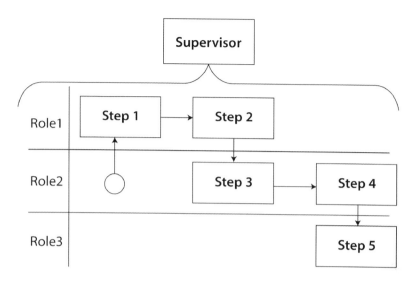

While it is acceptable to use the RACI model within a business process, it is equally acceptable to apply it to, or on, a business process. The difference between the two applications is significant and it makes a material difference in how each term is defined.

When applied to a process, RACI is used to define the architectural elements of the process rather than the transactional accountabilities within a process.

Consider the following scenario.

The managing director walks out of his office after losing a major tender. He turns to the sales director and asks, "Who designed the tender process? Who in their right mind thought that process would be suitable for us to win a tender?"

What he has not asked is, "Who filled in the tender response form? Who participated in the tender process?" Doing that would be to question the transactional aspects of the process. Rather his focus is on determining who the architect of the process was. Who designed the process, who approved it, and who can he hold accountable to ensure the process weakness is resolved and that the next tender is more successful?

Applying RACI on the process changes the definition of the terms as follows.

Responsible - accountable for designing the process.

Contribute - accountable for working with the Responsible person to design a process that was fit for purpose.

Informed - accountable for understanding how the new process works and how it impacts the informed manager's work environment.

Approve - accountable for signing off that the process is fit for purpose. That when it is followed, it will deliver optimal outcomes. This role owns that process.

In essence, the managing director is asking his team, "To what extent did you apply yourselves as senior managers to ensuring the process your staff were following, was fit for purpose?"

Using these definitions of RACI means that the supervisor (who was previously the Approver) now may become an informed party only and the manager's manager will approve the process.

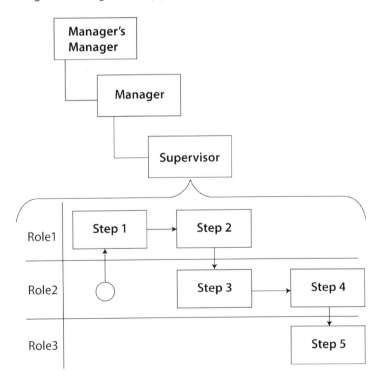

The supervisor's manager is more likely to be Responsible as the architect of the process. While the manager is Responsible for designing the process, it does not mean that they will necessarily do the work. Possibly they will delegate it back to the supervisor, but in this case, delegating the task does not equal delegating the accountability.

The two scenarios, in the process versus on the process, illustrate that depending on how RACI is applied, it will deliver very different levels of management accountability and they could be at opposite ends of the management spectrum. Supervisor versus manager's manager. Using the single term "Approve" for both situations is going to confuse the organisation and it raises the question: does the organisation want its processes approved by supervisors? It is reasonable to expect that this would not be the case.

The complexity between the two applications of RACI is increased when you consider that it is common for process flows to be modelled against roles and not positions. One position can play many roles. So when RACI is used in a process, it does not necessarily give accountability to a specific position. Rather, any position that happens be performing that role in that instance of the process becomes accountable. The burden this places on the organisation is significant. Just consider the training needs. Then there is the problem of process flows with process steps straddling the lines of responsibility or swim lanes and the issue of mixing roles and positions in process flows. These issues make defining accountability in the process level very confusing.

When RACI is applied on the process, it is applied to positions not roles thereby mitigating the above issue.

The difficulty of working with RACI is exponentially increased when applied to a matrix management organisation. Simplistically, matrix organisations can be broken down into service functions such as Human Resources, IT, Quality, Safety, Health, and Environment, Legal, and Finance, and the do work functions such as Operations, Work Winning, Logistics, Maintenance and Repair, and Customer Service. The service function will define the processes for the do work functions to use. A good example is the Quality, Safety, Health, and Environment function.

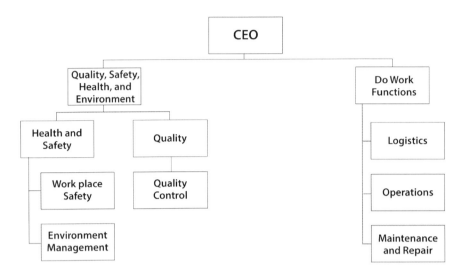

The processes defined by the Quality, Safety, Health, and Environment function are used on the shop floor by the do work teams. This means that the quality function is accountable for defining and approving quality management processes that will be used by a completely different function. The RACI model just doesn't cater for this level of sophistication. When you try and use it across the multiple silos of a matrix organisation it quickly becomes apparent that it just does not have enough variables to account for the organisational complexity and what is required is a different model for defining management accountability.

The best alternate model I have seen is the Linear Responsibility Matrix (LRM) methodology by Anthony Walker.

It is not my intention to repeat Anthony Walker's methodology here. What follows is my own interpretation of his methodology. I claim no rights to the methodology and I acknowledge Mr. Walker's ownership of the underlying intellectual property.

My interpretation of the LRM recognises ten functions with accountability. The original methodology had eleven.

1. Responsible
   ▪ Accountable for defining the process flow and associated artefacts.

2. Approve
   - Accountable for signing off the process flow and associated artefacts.
3. Contribute
   - Accountable for working with the Responsible person and helping design the process.
4. Informed
   - Accountable for being informed on how the process works and the requirements of any artefacts associated with the process.
5. General Oversight
   - Accountable for ensuring the process architecture is appropriate and fit for purpose.
6. Direct Oversight
   - Accountable for guiding the Responsible person.
7. Recommendation
   - Accountable for reviewing the process and ensuring it is fit for purpose. Once satisfied, this role endorses the process for final approval by the approver.
8. Monitor
   - Accountable for ensuring each instance of the process works as designed in the day- to-day environment.
9. Maintenance
   - Accountable for ensuring the process is being used as designed. It is quality control.
10. Boundary
    - Accountable for addressing areas of overlap in scope.

The word "process" in these definitions refers to the process appropriate to the level of management. At the senior level, it is the various value chains: Budget to Report, Contract to Cash, Procure to Pay, Hire to Retire etc. At the lower levels, the process is the transactional flow of a specific sequence of work. For senior management, the word "process" in the definitions can be substituted with specific items such as Policy or broader concepts such as the Governance Model for the organisation or a function.

This methodology is particularly powerful when working with matrix management organisations and the single biggest point to embrace is that the LRM is always on the process. It is never in the process.

In a matrix model, when it comes to defining the operating model for the service functions, the ten accountabilities can be loosely split between the service functions and the do work functions. On a per instance basis, this allocation could change.

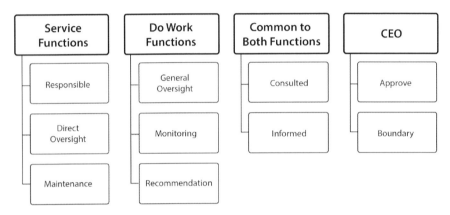

What this means is that the change program cannot work with each function in isolation of the other functions and importantly, the other functions do not have leeway to say, "Not my job." Rather the change agent should be establishing cross-functional teams based on the above separation of accountability to drive the change program and ensure the organisation gets a result that is sustainable and agreed.

Having ten functions with accountability gives the change agent a much wider scope for discussing the accountability of each and why senior management have no option but to become further involved in the business improvement program. You will note the first four functions with accountability largely correspond to RACI when RACI is applied on the process.

A senior manager would readily admit that when it comes to their function, the buck stops with them, but when pushed, it is often the case that these managers cannot easily describe what they are actually accountable for.

The ambiguity is because the names of functional areas (e.g. Quality, Safety, Health, and Environment) do not include verbs. Without a verb, defining the deliverable becomes very difficult. And if you can't describe the verb at the parent level, then defining the verb for the children and grandchildren levels becomes very difficult.

"Well, if you do that, then what do I do?"

I am not suggesting that the names of functional areas are rewritten to include verbs. Rather, for the purpose of defining management accountability, the verb is inferred. By agreeing the verb, you can agree the deliverable, and only then can you agree the management accountabilities.

For the function Quality, Safety, Health, and Environment consider the difference between the following two verb/deliverable combinations:

Verb	Deliverable
Monitor	The Quality, Safety, Health, and Environment governance model is working effectively.
Deliver	Quality, Safety, Health, and Environment is actively adopted throughout the organisation.
Transform	A new operating model for the Quality, Safety, Health, and Environment function is established.

It is accepted that the verb/deliverable combinations are not necessarily mutually exclusive and there is natural overlap between them. The verb sets up the focus for the function and will directly impact the way the function sees its role in the organisation and the culture that is established within the function.

The table can now be extended to bring in management accountability. Note how the accountability changes depending on the deliverable being sought.

		Position		
Verb	Deliverable	CEO	Quality, Safety, Health, and Environment Manager	Do Work Manager
Monitor	The Quality, Safety, Health, and Environment governance model is working effectively.	Approve	Responsible	General Oversight
Deliver	Quality, Safety, Health, and Environment is actively adopted throughout the organisation.	General Oversight	Approve	Responsible
Transform	A new operating model for the Quality, Safety, Health, and Environment function is established.	Recommends	Responsible	Consulted

When the verb is to monitor the Quality, Safety, Health, and Environment function, then the Quality, Safety, Health, and Environment manager cannot approve the deliverable as this would be a conflict of interest. In this case, using the reporting lines in the organisation chart above, only the CEO can approve that the Quality, Safety, Health, and Environment governance model is working effectively. At the senior levels, the do work manager will be watching proceedings to ensure the Quality, Safety, Health, and Environment governance model does not become an unnecessarily large administrative burden on the day-to-day operations of the business.

But if the verb was to deliver Quality, Safety, Health, and Environment, then the Quality, Safety, Health, and Environment manager could approve that the function was working as designed. This is because the deliverable has an operational focus and the senior Quality, Safety, Health, and Environment manager is expected to be the approver. It's part of the description of the position. The responsibility for delivering Quality, Safety, Health, and Environment on a day-to-day basis moves to the operations function as this is where the work actually happens.

If the verb was transform, then it is unlikely that the CEO would have the authority to approve the new operating model. This is where the LRM methodology really comes alive, as it brings in positions that sit outside the obvious reporting lines and the function accountability table needs to extend to allow for the additional accountabilities.

		Position							
Verb	Deliverable	Board	CEO	Quality, Safety, Health, and Environment Manager	Quality Manager	Do Work Manager	Legal	Country Manager	ISO Authority
Monitor	The Quality Safety, Health, and Environment governance model is working effectively	Monitor	Approve	Responsible	Consulted	General Oversight	Recommends	Recommends	Consulted
Deliver	Quality Safety, Health, and Environment is actively adopted throughout the organisation		General Oversight	Approve	Maintenance	Responsible		Monitor	
Transform	A new operating model for the Quality, Safety, Health, and Environment function is established	Approve	Recommends	Responsible	Informed	Consulted	Consulted	Consulted	Consulted

For transform, the Board is now accountable for approving the new operating model for Quality, Safety, Health, and Environment. The CEO can only recommend the new model up for approval, but they will not do so unless they know the senior team has been consulted on the design of the new model.

For deliver, the quality manager is accountable for maintaining the integrity of the Quality processes within the organisation. The senior do work manager is responsible for ensuring the do work function are using the Quality, Safety, Health, and Environment processes across the entire organisation and, in this example, the country manager is accountable for monitoring that the Quality, Safety, Health, and Environment processes are being followed on a daily basis.

For monitor, the CEO is unlikely to approve the governance model unless it is recommended to him for approval by the legal counsel and the country manager. Recommending it for approval implies that they have reviewed it in detail and consider it fit for purpose.

The LRM model is also useful for defining accountabilities within a function.

The following uses the Quality, Safety, Health, and Environment structure referred to above. It has four levels.

The table illustrates how the accountability for Approve and Responsible changes as you move to the lower levels in the organisation.

Level	CEO	Manager's Manager	Manager	Supervisor
Organisational Level-2	Approve	Responsible		
Organisational Level-3		Approve	Responsible	
Organisational Level-4				Monitor

Each organisational level requires a verb and a deliverable and there should be a natural relationship of deliverables between the organisational levels. It is implied that the accountability of other relevant positions will be included as required.

It is important that Responsible is not delegated below manager level and accountability for Approval is held at the level of manager's manager or higher.

Organisational level 4 is typically the transactional level in an organisation. This is the level where the business process is operationalised. This requires the supervisor to monitor the process to ensure it is working as defined and correct it as required when the process deviates from design. Maintenance by comparison would be carried out by a representative of the function that designed the process. For example, Quality or Safety.

It is not necessary to recognise all ten accountabilities for each function or process as it will make the model overly complex and confusing. Rather, it is easier to work with the implied hierarchy between the accountabilities and use the dominant accountability. For example, there is no need to state that a manager who is recommending a process for approval is also informed. It stands to reason that they would not recommend something they were not informed on. The same applies for consulted and recommend. It is highly unlikely a manager would be asked to recommend a model they had not been consulted on, in the definition phase.

When defining which positions require to be informed, the "less is more" principle is relevant. Sure, everybody needs to know about changes, but these changes will be rolled out through the organisation structure. All that is required is to define which managers must be formally informed of the changes.

What these management accountability models achieve is to cause the business to change itself.

Without this level of accountability, the responsibility for the success of the change program will, in practice, fall back to the change team, allowing management to point fingers and attribute blame for failure. There is no doubt that change will take longer to achieve when management are correctly held to account, but equally, there is no doubt that the benefits will be sustainable and owned by management when they are forced to be actively involved throughout the change journey.

Stakeholder Motivation

I am frequently asked to write on the mechanics of change management, a level of detail I have tried hard to avoid until now. The reason is simple—change management is complex, it is difficult, and it should not be reduced to a series of "cookie cutter" activities. I will never understand why large business improvement programs frequently refuse to pay a decent wage for the change manager's role. On less than successful programs, it is common to hear statements to the effect of "the change management work stream failed" or "we would have delivered a better program if we had started the change piece earlier" or other words similar in nature. These statements assume that the business improvement program had any change management at all. Frequently, this is not the case.

No doubt, each unsuccessful program would have involved the completion of a stakeholder analysis, the delivery of training, and the publishing of communications. But I doubt all of these were delivered in a cohesive, integrated broadside to the organisation. I use the word "broadside" deliberately. Treating these as activities is why business improvement programs fail to deliver the required changes in organisational behaviour. Activities tend to get completed sequentially and then signed off as complete when delivered. In this case, the business improvement program has, at best, a change coordinator. "We have done the stakeholder analysis."—tick.

When it comes to change, the most fundamental question to ask is: so what? What has been learnt from a change activity? What is the business going to do with the information?

Note that the question does not ask what the program team is going to do with the information. That is of lesser importance than what the business is going to do with it. This distinction is vital, as the program team cannot change the business. Only the business (line management) can change the business. The program team will do all the heavy lifting required to meet the agreed deliverables. It just won't change the business. If the business does not want to change, then the program office, despite its best efforts, will deliver a sub-optimal result and the senior management team will once again wonder what went wrong. By the time they realise that they have abdicated their responsibility for achieving a successful outcome, it will be too late to make corrections without the need to invest significantly more money into the program than what was budgeted for. Effective stakeholder management substantially reduces this risk.

Effective stakeholder management starts with the program sponsor. The sponsor is accountable for achieving the business benefits and this, by necessity, must include accountability for the change management work stream. Consider: if the business was serious about improvement, then it would hardly make sense to make a support function (change manager) accountable for achieving the structural and cultural change necessary to deliver the desired business benefits. The change manager's role then becomes one of a subject matter expert designated to guide the sponsor through the difficulties associated with change. This would not exempt the change manager from their responsibility to prepare traditional deliverables such as impact studies, training packs, communications, etc.

A primary variable in any change program is people's behaviour, as individuals and as groups, and the key objective of the change program is to establish predictability of behaviour. Predictability cuts both ways. The change program must provide predictability to those staff impacted by the change so they know what to expect, and equally the change manager, working through the sponsor, must provide management with predictability of how those staff will respond to the change and what is required from them as a senior leadership group. When people know what to expect, then they will be more accepting of the change when it happens, even if the change has a negative impact on them.

In practice, predictability and stakeholder management are synonymous terms and this means stakeholder management moves from being a discrete task in a change management plan to being the backbone of all the change management activities. To further illustrate this point, consider the following typical change management plan.

Change Activity	Month 1	Month 2	Month 3	Month 4	Month 5	Month 6
1. Develop Change Management Strategy and Plan	•					
2. Develop Change Impact Assessment	•					
3. Develop Stakeholder Management Plan	•					
4. Develop Communications Plan		•				
5. Develop Communications		•				
6. Develop Training Plan		•				
7. Develop Training Material					•	
8. Develop Change Readiness Assessment					•	
9. Develop Change Management Schedule (integral with program)		•				
10 Deliver Stakeholder Management Plan		•	•	•	•	•
11 Deliver Communications		•	•	•	•	•
12 Deliver Training						•
13 Deliver Change Readiness Assessment					•	•
14 Manage Change Management		•	•	•	•	•

To actively manage stakeholders requires agreement on who the stakeholders are. A stakeholder impact analysis workshop will help to identify the extended set of stakeholders. Stakeholders can be individuals or groups. For example, the CFO is part of the executive team, a key stakeholder group, and yet the CFO is important enough for the role to be identified as its own stakeholder group. In this way the CFO is referenced twice in the stakeholder management plan.

The impact analysis is a determination of how widely the "ripples" of the business improvement program will be felt. Ripples are typically operational, financial, or reputational. I define these terms in the broadest possible way.

The above methodology table indicates that the impact analysis is completed prior to the stakeholder management workshop. In practice, the two activities are iterative as each informs the other.

Once the stakeholder groups are identified, then the next step is to determine the best means to engage with each group, to bring them into the change program and cause them to actively participate. Basic psychology says that this is best achieved by engaging them on topics that interest them, in a manner that interests them. To this end a simple 2x2 matrix that cross references Power (the capability to influence the direction or outcome of the program) to Interest (the desire to influence the direction or outcome of the program) is a frequently used methodology.

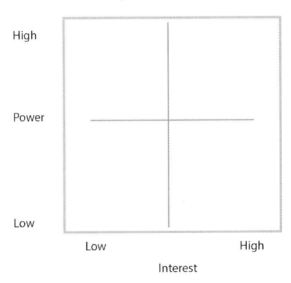

This type of analysis is only valuable if the terms Power and Interest are understood. In her article posted on the American Express OPEN forum, (https://www.americanexpress.com/us/small-business/openforum/s/?query=Nicole%20Lipkin%20) psychologist Nicole Lipkin discusses seven types of power, namely:

Legitimate Power is where a person in a higher position has control over people in a lower position in an organisation.

"If you have this power, it's essential that you understand that this power was given to you (and can be taken away), so don't abuse it," Lipkin says. "If Diane rises to the position of CEO and her employees believe she deserves this position, they will respond favourably when she exercises her legitimate power. On the other hand, if Diane rises to the position of

CEO, but people don't believe that she deserves this power, it will be a bad move for the company as a whole."

Coercive Power is where a person leads by threats and force. It is unlikely to win respect and loyalty from employees for long.

"There is not a time of day when you should use it," Lipkin tells us. "Ultimately, you can't build credibility with coercive influence—you can think of it like bullying in the workplace."

Expert Power is the result of the perception that one possesses superior skills or knowledge.

"If Diane holds an MBA and a PhD in statistical analysis, her colleagues and reports are more inclined to accede to her expertise," Lipkin says.

In order to keep their status and influence, however, experts need to continue learning and improving.

Informational Power is where a person possesses needed or wanted information. This is a short- term power that doesn't necessarily influence or build credibility.

For example, a program manager may have all the information for a specific program, and that will give her "informational power." But it's hard for a person to keep this power for long, and eventually this information will be released. This should not be a long-term strategy.

Reward Power is where a person motivates others by offering raises, promotions, and awards.

"When you start talking financial livelihood, power takes on a whole new meaning," Lipkin says. For example, "both Diane and Bob hold a certain amount of reward power if they administer performance reviews that determine raises and bonuses for their people."

Connection Power is where a person attains influence by gaining favour or simply acquaintance with a powerful person. This power is all about networking.

"If I have a connection with someone that you want to get to, that's going to give me power. That's politics in a way," Lipkin says. "People employing this power build important coalitions with others ... Diane's natural ability to forge such connections with individuals and assemble them into coalitions gives her strong connection power."

Referent Power is the ability to convey a sense of personal acceptance or approval. It is held by people with charisma, integrity, and other positive qualities. It is the most valuable type of power.

The most frequently used definition of power is legitimate power and using this definition alone is short-sighted. Staff who have relatively low legitimate power can have very high power when it comes to influencing the success of the program. This is especially true for subject matter experts who have expert power.

Once you consider all seven types of power, then it is likely that the set of identified stakeholder groups will be refined and expanded.

Equally, Interest can have multiple variables. I recommend using the same as those used to determine the "ripples" in the impact analysis, namely:

Operational Interest is a primary focus on structure, strategy, environment, and implementation; a desire to improve the operational effectiveness and efficiency of the business.

Financial Interest is a primary focus on the ROI and the impact on the balance sheet.

Reputational Interest is a primary focus on the company's reputation in the market or the individual stakeholder's own brand value.

Typically, all three variables will apply to each stakeholder group, but each group will have a leaning to one or another of them. For example, a middle manager will have a high interest in the operational benefits of the program and a lower interest in the financial aspects. They get their salary no matter what, so financially the program may not change their situation much, but operationally, the program could materially impact their work environment.

Then there is a forth variable to interest—self-interest.

Self-Interest is a primary focus on oneself. The WIIFM question or "what's in it for me?" How will the program impact an individual's personal circumstances?

This analysis gets interesting when it is used to evaluate how the nature of a stakeholder group's interest will change depending on the health of the program.

To fully consider the relationship between the power and interest variables, it makes more sense to use a table rather than a simple 2x2 grid.

Stakeholder Group	Sensitivity Analysis 1 = Highest priority 4 = Lowest priority	Power (Nature of Influence)							
		Legitimate Power is where a person in a higher position has control over people in a lower position in an organisation.				Expert Power is the perception that one possesses superior skills or knowledge.			
		Area of Interest (1=H,4=Low)							
		Financial	Operational	Reputational	Self-Interest	Financial	Operational	Reputational	Self-Interest
Executive Management	Project is healthy	1	3	2	4				
	Project is experiencing difficulties	2	1	3	4				
	Project is in substantial trouble	3	2	1	4				
Subject Matter Expert	Project is healthy					3	1	2	4
	Project is experiencing difficulties					3	1	4	2
	Project is in substantial trouble					4	3	2	1

In this example, "Executive Management" has legitimate power with a primary interest in the financial results of the program. They are focused on ensuring the program is on budget and is delivering the promised ROI. They will also want to be sure that the change program is enhancing or has a neutral impact on the reputation of the company. As they are senior managers, they are less interested in the day-to-day operations and should be least worried about their "Self-Interest." Obviously, depending on the specific circumstances of any given change program, the priority between the four interest types will change.

The above prioritisation should remain true while the business improvement program is going well. It will change if the health of the program declines and starts to have an adverse impact on business operations. When this happens, executive management will want to ensure that the business can still run and consequently, they will become less worried about delivering the program on budget. Their primary interest will switch from "Financial" to "Operational" and they will start to release additional funds. "Financial Interest" is reprioritised to second place and "Reputation" moves to third.

If the program health declines further, they may switch their primary interest to "Reputation" and start to take action to ensure reputational damage is minimised and operations are stabilised. "Financial Interest" moves to third priority.

In these examples, I have left "Self-Interest" at priority four, assuming that the executives are all professionals. It is realistic, however, to believe that individual executives will start to reprioritise self-interest higher up the scale depending on their exposure to the consequences of a failed program.

By comparison, the stakeholder group "Subject Matter Expert" is characterised by technically competent staff who are experts in their field. This group will typically have a high "Operational Interest" in the program, especially if it relies on their expertise and enhances their reputation ("Reputational Interest"). They will also want the business reputation to grow as it helps their CV. These staff may never rise to the senior levels of management and are less interested in "Financials." Stereotypically, as long as the company keeps funding their budget they are happy. With a healthy program, their "Self-Interest" is the lowest priority.

If the program health declines, then their Self-Interest will very quickly get reprioritised to the top of the list, as a subject matter expert typically does not want to be associated with a failed program, particularly in their area of speciality.

As the program health changes, so should the mode of the interaction the program has with each stakeholder group.

The 2x2 matrix can now be used as a guide to determine the best means of interacting with a specific stakeholder group with the caveat that Power is changed to Power type and Interest is changed to Interest type and the message is tailored to suit.

The quadrant into which a stakeholder falls, dictates the suite of preferred interaction styles that could be used to engage with that stakeholder. Interaction types include:

- One-to-one interactions
- One-to-few
- One-to-many
- Email
- Town-hall meetings
- Theatre
- Website updates
- Intranet forums (chat rooms)
- Awareness education
- Workshops
- Delegations of authority*
- Technical training
- Posters, brochures, and other marketing collateral.

* Delegations of authority refers to the degree to which a position or role can make a decision that will bind the company. Pushing delegation levels lower into the company should result in higher levels of involvement in the program as the applicable manager responds to the fact that they can make a meaningful and sustainable difference to the change program.

It should be noted that all types of interaction are relevant. What changes is the importance and reliance that should be placed on a specific type as a means to effectively engage a specific stakeholder group, with a realisation that the most effective mode will change with the health of the program.

Subject matter experts will probably respond to detailed website updates and awareness education sessions far better than to face-to-face meetings. Executives, on the other hand, will most likely respond better to succinct emails and face-to-face briefings. Tied to this, is the content of the interaction. As a stakeholder's interest changes with the health of the program, so should the content covered in each interaction.

The matrix now looks as follows:

	Low	High
High	One-to-few Email Website updates Awareness education Posters, brochures, and other marketing collateral	One-to-few Email Website updates Intranet forums Awareness education Participation in workshops Delegations of authority Posters, brochures, and other marketing collateral
Low	One-to-many Email Town-hall meetings Website updates Posters, brochures, and other marketing collateral	One-to-many Email Town-hall meetings Theatre Website updates Intranet forums Awareness education Participation in workshops Posters, brochures, and other marketing collateral

Power type (vertical axis: High / Low)
Interest type (horizontal axis: Low / High)

I close with a reinforcement of the principle that only the business can change itself and that the change manager must ensure that their activities do not absolve the sponsor and other key stakeholders from their accountability to make the program successful.

The Importance of Optics

Common wisdom tells us that if something looks like a duck, walks like a duck, and talks like a duck, then most likely, it is a duck. We all know, however, that this is not always true.

The idea of optics is captured perfectly in a scene from the movie "The Tuxedo." Jackie Chan is working for a millionaire and in the scene the millionaire turns to Jackie and says, "It's 90% the suit."

What he is referring to is the optics of a situation—what perception the picture creates.

In Australian politics, the Federal Treasurer, Mr. Joe Hockey, was photographed smoking a cigar at the time when he was bringing down a tough budget in parliament. The imagery was all wrong and the press had a field day depicting Mr. Hockey as a fat cat, smoking cigars while the common man battled. The depiction was completely unfair and most people knew it, but it was an association Mr. Hockey was never able to fully shake.

Optics is the non-verbal, subliminal messaging that surrounds the actual message. When it comes to stakeholder management, optics is central to everything. It is the backbone to effective communications.

Optics are why politicians kiss a baby whenever there is a camera about. They are demonstrating their support for families and that they are in touch with the community. It is most certainly not because they like kissing babies.

A key feature of optics is that they are primarily associated with a person or a business and are not time sensitive. It is common for people to unconsciously develop a view of a person over a period of time simply by watching how they handle themselves in and around the office. This will include how they dress, the hours they work, or even their punctuality at meetings.

What this means is that, when it comes to stakeholder management, what you do and what you don't do, and how and when you say something are as important as what you say, and possibly even more important.

The best example I have of this is a client I worked with a few years ago. He asked for me to analyse a significant body of data. This assignment was beyond my skillset and I invited a colleague to join the project to complete this piece of work. My colleague had a PhD in Physics and was undoubtedly the best person for the job. Unfortunately, he also had numerous tattoos and body piercings. My client was unable to see past the earrings and tattoos and requested that he be removed from the project. I argued that he was a PhD and was highly professional. My client was unrepentant. He was unwilling to accept that a person who looked like my colleague could ever produce a creditable outcome. He was concerned that if the project outcome was suboptimal, then he would be blamed for giving the work to such a person.

The words "What were you thinking?" were already ringing in his ears.

Optics can extend beyond the person to the theatre in which the message is delivered. When Tony Abbott was shadow prime minister he spoke at a political rally. I don't remember what he was talking about, but I clearly remember him standing in front of various signboards that said "Ditch the witch" and similar slogans. The slogans all referred to the then Prime Minister Ms. Julia Gillard and while these slogans had nothing to do with Mr. Abbott, he did make the decision to stand in front of them. His poor choice of theatre gave Ms. Gillard significant political capital and she went on to portray Mr. Abbott as someone who disrespected women and consistently brought up his apparent misogyny at every opportunity. There was not a lot Mr Abbott could do in response, as he had put himself in front of the signs. The message he delivered that day was lost, dwarfed by the poor choice of the theatre in which he chose to deliver the message. The optics of that day were just wrong.

Optics generally refer to the perception that a person creates by their behaviour, dress, and choice of presentation theatre. The term can also subsequently extend to the spoken word. I say subsequently as the audience will already have formed an impression about the speaker long before the person starts to speak. I witnessed this firsthand when I was working with a senior IT executive. We had arranged for a supplier to showcase their solution. Unfortunately, the presenter was young and he pronounced the word "something" as "somethink." He also said "yous" when referring to my client's company. The combination of youth and pronunciation errors irritated my client so much he stopped listening to what the person was saying and worried only about how he was saying it. The relationship with the supplier died in that meeting. My client felt disrespected and that his time had been wasted. It is worth noting that had my client wanted to buy expertise on social media, then the presenter's youth probably would have been an asset.

The take out is that effective stakeholder management requires the speaker to look the part, sound the part, and to manage the theatre in which the message is delivered.

This can include everything from how a person dresses to how long they took to prepare a presentation. Consider a manager going out to a factory to address the staff. If they wear a suit and cuff links, the factory staff will find it difficult to see past the suit and hear the message. All they will see is a stuffed shirt coming from head office to give them news they assume they don't want to hear.

Equally, if the manager arrived wearing factory uniform, the staff would question who the manager was trying to impress. They might reject the approach, and say, "You are not one of us." Once again, the message would be discounted.

There is no right answer. It really depends on the message. If it is bad news, I would counsel the manager not to stand behind a table or lectern or on a stage. Rather they should stand in front of the staff with no barriers and no ceremony. The manager will look sincere and will have a much better chance of being heard. After addressing the staff, the manager should leave through the same door as the staff, at the same time. All these cues will reinforce the subliminal message the manager respects the staff and sees them as equals.

The opposite can hold true when addressing a senior audience. In this case the manager should wear a tie, have polished shoes, and be on time. When the manager enters the room, the senior team will immediately make a judgement on the quality of the information they are about to hear. The quality of the presentation is important. It should look like the presenter took the time to do a good job. A great message poorly portrayed will have less traction with the stakeholders than a well-presented weaker message.

Managing the optics is especially important when a country suffers a natural disaster. An unfortunate but excellent example is how the U.S. federal government responded to Hurricane Katrina.

You will recall that in the days and weeks after Katrina flattened New Orleans and the surrounding countryside, the world's press beamed live pictures of people who had lost everything. The implication was that the government had failed in its duties. The press repeatedly asked, "When is help coming? Why weren't people warned? Etc

The optics were that the government was caught napping, was incompetent, and indifferent. In the lessons learnt document published in the months following Katrina, the author notes:

On September 1, conflicting views of New Orleans emerged with positive statements by some Federal officials that contradicted a more desperate picture painted by reporters in the streets. The media, operating 24/7, gathered and aired uncorroborated information which interfered with ongoing emergency response efforts. http://library.stmarytx.edu/acadlib/edocs/katrinawh.pdf

The truth of the matter is that the local, state, and federal administrations had put substantial preparation and risk mitigation strategies into place prior to the storm. The media ignored this and only presented half the story.

This example reinforces the point that the optics created about you or your company can be created just as much by a third party as they can be by you. And no matter who creates them, or how accurate they are, they do need to be managed.

My mom taught me not to judge a book by its cover. I would love to say I don't, but I know that I do. We all do. In business terms, when it comes to successfully managing stakeholders, it is essential that you are highly sensitive to your "cover" and that you manage the perception it creates. Fail to do this and your audience may never take the time to really listen to what you have to say.

The problem is that you can only do what you can do. The stereotypes, bigotry, baggage, biases, and cultural differences that your audience brings with them are largely beyond your control. I say largely because you can still mitigate for these hidden filters with some consideration of who your stakeholders are and what they represent.

If you are talking to an older audience, you should expect them to be more conservative and unlikely to make a quick decision. If you are talking to women, then swearing is unlikely to be well received. Equally, a young underdressed female presenter is unlikely to get a warm reception from senior executives, male or female. Engineers are generally detail people. They will forgive a few faux pas if the presenter knows their topic in detail. By contrast, senior managers do not want detail. German audiences respect formal dress and titles and Japanese audiences respect the past. Younger audiences are more receptive to a technology demonstration and frequently less hung up on the formalities that senior audiences appreciate. Having said that, it would be a mistake not to take a young audience seriously.

For each one of these examples, there will be folks immediately quoting examples that contradict me. That's to be expected because when it comes to stakeholder management, you have to deal with individuals and known groups. Stereotypes may not apply.

The take out is this. Always respect the theatre in which you work.

Stakeholder Impact Analysis

Consultants and other business advisors are frequently brought in by senior management to establish and lead a change program within the business. This brings to mind an old joke. How many consultants does it take to change a light bulb? Just one, but the light bulb has to want to change. An old joke for sure, but it reinforces the inescapable truth that a consultant cannot change a business. Only the business can change the business. If the business does not want to change, then there is nothing the consultant can do.

But who is the business? The business is a collection of people working together to achieve a common objective. For change to be successful, these same people need to band together to build a momentum for change that cannot be stopped. The organisation must push over the tipping point to make change inevitable.

The problem is that, in large organisations, whilst most staff support the overall business objectives, they don't necessarily agree on the best way to achieve them. A characteristic of large organisations is the proliferation of subcultures throughout the business. These subcultures are normally aligned to the different stakeholder communities or silos that make up the business. Depending on the specifics of each subculture, change will be met with a range of mindsets. Some will say, "I have been here fifteen years and I've seen it all before. It didn't work then and it won't work now." Others will say, "If it ain't broke, don't fix it." And still others will say, "We welcome the opportunity to change."

For change to be successful, these individual communities need to be recognised, understood, and engaged as stakeholders in the change program. The trick is identifying each different stakeholder community and determining how change will individually and collectively impact each community and how each will respond to the proposed changes.

This paper will not discuss in detail how to identify individual stakeholder groups. Rather, it will examine how to evaluate the impact of a change program on stakeholder groups and how these same groups can impact the change program.

It is common practice to start an impact analysis with a stakeholder identification exercise, the rationale being that once you know who the stakeholders are, you can evaluate the impact change will have on them. My experience is that an effective stakeholder impact analysis must start with an analysis of the impact of change on the business. After all, how can you be confident that you have identified the complete and correct set of stakeholders, never mind the impact of change on these stakeholders, until you have fully understood the impact change will have on the business as a whole?

I have found that while most change practitioners agree with the above, they also frequently attempt to complete both analyses at the same time. Inevitably, this will deliver a skewed and incomplete result. It is important to complete the studies sequentially.

To understand the business impact, it is easiest to use the traditional variables of people, process, and technology, with the addition of foundation items such as culture, strategy, policy, and rules.

Collectively, these variables will provide the necessary width to complete a suitably comprehensive business impact analysis.

The objective of the study is to agree what will be different in the business as a result of the change. The framework overleaf can assist.

Foundation

Culture
* The business moves away from service delivery to vendor management.
* Staff and managers will be required to improve their planning disciplines.

Strategy
* Focus on client service delivery, not production.
* Implement best practice disciplines and processes.

Policy
* No new policies will be introduced in the short term.

Rules
* No new rules will be introduced.

Technology

Information Access
* Additional wireless access points in more locations.
* Cloud-based architecture.
* Flatter, simpler network.

Information
* 99.95% availability with 24x7 support across three global time zones.
* Real-time update on incident ticket status.

Applications
* Sharepoint
* Office 365
* Business management system
* Document management system

Process

Flow
* No fundamental change to business process.
* Reduced flexibility to work outside of process.
* New incident management process for severity 1 and 2 tickets.

Management Practice
* Requirement is to hold vendor responsible for service quality based on contracted SLAs.
* Business to retain management accountability for client outcomes.

Organisation Chart
* Flatter organisation structure.
* Improved alignment within matrix structure.

People

Names
* There will be reduction in the availability of in-house technical skills.

Positions
* There will be reduction in the number of positions available.
* Positions will be transferred to services provider.

Roles
* Move to a vendor management role rather than a delivery role.
* Vendor will assume responsibility for all level 2 support.

The table is a summary of the impact of change on the business.

You will note that the framework breaks the headers of people, process, technology into their component parts. It is the component parts that are analysed, not the header itself.

A key part of any change program is effective communication in order to ensure senior managers understand the need for change. To be successful, it is vital that a senior stakeholder is able to quickly assimilate and understand the issues. It is not uncommon for an overly detailed analysis to be put in the "too hard basket," causing the findings to be partially ignored or even lost entirely.

If the table is detailed, it can be supplemented with Harvey Balls to provide a quick summary of the extent of the change.

Dark (red) indicates a high degree of change.

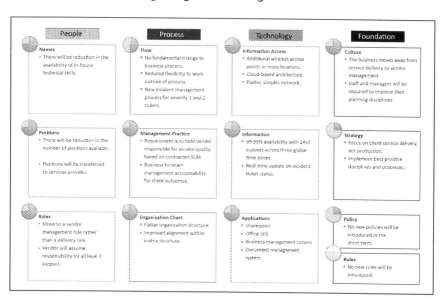

Using the Harvey Balls as a guide, it can be seen that the proposed changes will have a moderate impact on the business processes and a high impact on people, management practice, structure, and culture. There will be limited impact on strategy, policy, and business rules.

This summary is highly significant, as the common practice in business improvement programs is to map the business processes. In this case, understanding the business processes may be important, but it is not where the real game is. Rather, a strong focus on people and culture is more likely to deliver the desired business benefits. The detail in each cell describes the nature of the change.

Depending on its size, a change program will comprise multiple projects or work streams, each focusing on a different aspect of change such as Quality, HR, IT, or operational improvements.

The framework can be used for each project within the program. As before, Harvey Balls can be used to indicate the magnitude of the change within each project.

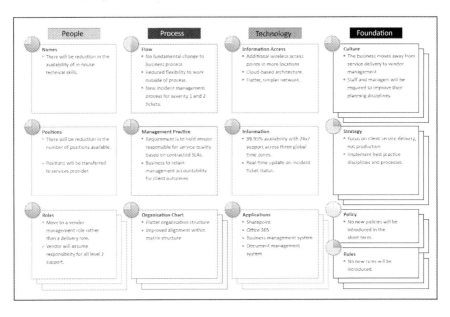

This type of analysis will provide a manager with a ready snapshot of the impact of each project's specific changes on the business. While this view is valuable, it is incomplete.

What is required is a consolidated picture of change across all projects.

	People		Process		Technology	Culture
Project	People	Flow	Management Practice	Organisation Chart	Access to Information	Culture
Project 1	◕	◑	◕	◕	◕	◕
Project 2	◕	◑	◕	◕	◔	◕
Project 3	⬤	◕	⬤	⬤	⬤	⬤
Project 4	◑	◑	◕	○	◑	◕
Project 5	◕	◕	◕	◕	◕	◕

The table provides a consolidated and immediate insight into how the projects will individually and collectively impact the business. You will note that the subcategories of "people" have been removed. This is to support the principle of "easy to understand." Senior stakeholders will want to know how much change will impact their people. The fine detail is unlikely to be important at this time.

In the example, project 3 is anticipated to have the biggest impact across the entire business, and management practice, access to information, and culture will be most heavily impacted across all projects.

	People		Process		Technology	Culture
Project	People	Flow	Management Practice	Organisation Chart	Access to Information	Culture
Project 1	◕	◑	◕	◕	◕	◕
Project 2	◕	◑	◕	◕	◕	◕
Project 3	⬤	◕	⬤	⬤	⬤	⬤
Project 4	◑	◑	◕	○	◑	◕
Project 5	◕	◕	◕	◕	◕	◕

This table now becomes the basis for determining the real stakeholder groups. Given that process flows are not a top three priority, it is unlikely that the process operators are going to be a primary stakeholder. Conversely, their managers are identified as a primary stakeholder. This is reinforced when you consider management's impact on culture and access to information.

With this insight, the change program can set its priorities and tailor the messaging appropriately.

To understand how the change program will impact a specific stakeholder group requires the application of a consistent numerical scale. Such a scale could be:

0 – No impact
1 – Low impact
2 – Moderate impact
3 – High impact
4 – Maximum impact

Each stakeholder group is then evaluated according to this scale and the results are tabulated as follows. The stakeholders are listed down the page. The types of change the stakeholders will go through are listed across the top of the table. Once again the variables of people, process, and technology are used to guide the analysis. It is unlikely that the detail will be a mirror of the business impact table, but it is expected that the business impact table will inform the variables used in this study.

Legend	No impact 0	Low 1	Moderate 2	High 3	Max 4					
	People						Process			
	Learn new skills	Recruitment	Adopt new behaviour	Introduce new policies	Introduce new processes	Changes to management controls	Introduce active measures	New reporting ines	Use new technnology	
Stakeholder										Totals
Stakeholder group 1	4	1	4	4	4	4	4	4	4	33
Stakeholder group 2	4	1	4	4	4	4	3	4	4	32
Stakeholder group 3	3	3	4	4	3	4	3	3	3	30
Stakeholder group 4	2	0	4	2	3	4	4	4	4	27
Stakeholder group 5	2	0	3	1	4	4	4	4	4	26
Stakeholder group 6	2	0	3	1	4	4	4	4	4	26
Stakeholder group 7	2	0	3	1	4	2	4	4	4	24
Stakeholder group 8	3	0	4	0	3	4	3	3	3	23
Stakeholder group 9	2	0	2	1	4	3	4	3	3	22
Stakeholder group 10	2	0	3	3	3	3	1	2	4	21
Stakeholder group 11	2	0	2	3	2	1	3	3	3	19
Stakeholder group 12	2	0	2	3	3	3	1	3	2	19
Stakeholder group 13	1	1	2	3	3	2	2	2	2	18
Stakeholder group 14	1	0	1	3	3	3	1	3	3	18
Stakeholder group 15	2	0	3	1	3	1	2	2	2	16
Stakeholder group 16	2	0	3	1	3	1	2	2	2	16
Stakeholder group 17	1	0	1	2	2	3	4	0	1	14
Stakeholder group 18	1	0	1	2	3	1	3	0	0	11
Stakeholder group 19	2	2	1	2	1	1	1	1	1	12
Stakeholder group 20	1	0	1	1	2	1	3	1	1	11
Stakeholder group 21	1	0	1	0	1	1	2	2	2	10
Stakeholder group 22	1	0	3	2	1	0	1	1	1	10
Stakeholder group 23	1	0	1	1	1	1	1	1	1	8
Stakeholder group 24	1	4	0	2	0	0	0	0	0	7
Stakeholder group 25	1	0	3	1	1	0	1	0	0	7
Stakeholder group 26	0	0	2	1	0	0	2	1	1	7
Stakeholder group 27	0	0	1	2	0	0	1	1	0	5
	46	12	62	51	65	55	64	58	59	

The table is completed once the totals column is complete. To really make sense of the table, graph it and rank it from highest impact to lowest. It is clear that the first six stakeholder groups will be most impacted by the program and the last four stakeholder groups will be least impacted.

The primary difference between the stakeholders on the left-hand side of the graph and those on the right is that those on the left will typically be operational staff and those on the right will be senior managers and executives. The seniority of these managers means that they are unlikely to be substantially impacted by the technical aspects of the change program.

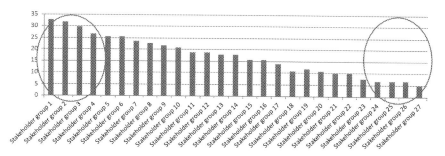

This type of stakeholder analysis is common practice and in the normal course of events, the change program would target the top six with specific interventions and deal with the bottom four with general interventions. The stakeholders in between would gradually move from specific to general.

By general activity, I refer to interventions aimed at groups, rather than individuals. It would be brilliant if a company had the time and resources to work with each person in the company individually. This luxury is seldom, if ever, open to large companies and so change is addressed with general activities.

My critique is that this is a one-way study, in that it only evaluates how the change program impacts the stakeholders.

In my opinion, a far more critical analysis is an evaluation of how the same set of stakeholders could impact the success of the change program through their actions, be they positive or negative, or simply through inaction.

The point of this second study is to determine which individual stakeholder groups could substantially impact the success of the project if they wanted to. Consider: if the executive team chose to, they could terminate a specific project or even the entire program, a particularly substantial impact. If the service desk became disenchanted, they could reduce the quality of the customer service they provide. This would dilute all the good work done on the rest of the project. It would not stop the project, but it would have a detrimental effect on customer satisfaction.

To complete this study, the scoring can again be on a simple low to high scale, as the evaluation is more subjective than objective.

1: No impact
2: Low impact
3: Medium impact
4: High impact

When completing the analysis to determine how stakeholders could impact the change program, it is important to use the same stakeholders that were evaluated in the first study.

Influence on project

Stakeholder group 1	4
Stakeholder group 2	4
Stakeholder group 3	4
Stakeholder group 4	4
Stakeholder group 5	1
Stakeholder group 6	1
Stakeholder group 7	1
Stakeholder group 8	4
Stakeholder group 9	1
Stakeholder group 10	1
Stakeholder group 11	3
Stakeholder group 12	1
Stakeholder group 13	3
Stakeholder group 14	2
Stakeholder group 15	4
Stakeholder group 16	4
Stakeholder group 17	1
Stakeholder group 18	1
Stakeholder group 19	3
Stakeholder group 20	4
Stakeholder group 21	1
Stakeholder group 22	1
Stakeholder group 23	1
Stakeholder group 24	1
Stakeholder group 25	3
Stakeholder group 26	4
Stakeholder group 27	4

As before, the scores are graphed. It is important that the stakeholder sequence is kept constant as per the first graph.

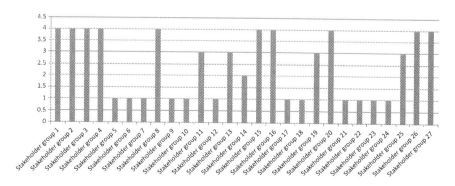

It can be seen that, unlike the initial study that produced a smooth graph, this study produces a saw- toothed result, indicating that there are stakeholders across the full spectrum that can significantly impact the project.

Of particular interest are the stakeholders on the right. In the first graph these stakeholders were scored very low as they were deemed to be senior or executive managers and therefore largely unaffected by the technical aspects of change. But in this second graph, they have a very high score as they have the position and power to substantially impact the project.

The full strength of the analysis is evident when the two graphs are compared.

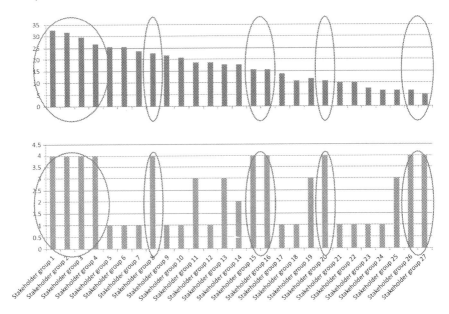

As expected, there is a strong two-way impact across the first four stakeholder groups. These are the primary stakeholders impacted by the project and, if they are not fully enlisted in the change program, then it will be almost impossible to achieve sustainable business improvements.

Equally, when looking only at the first graph, it is unlikely that stakeholder groups 8 and 9 would have been considered particularly important stakeholder groups. But when combined with the second graph, they become high priority stakeholders.

The first graph is an analysis of the technical aspects of the change program. It evaluates which stakeholders will be impacted by the change and the data behind the graph will tell you why they are impacted. In many respects, change will happen to these stakeholders whether they want it or not. This does not diminish the responsibility of the change manager to minimise their resistance to change as much as possible.

By comparison, the second graph reflects the political aspects of the change. While these stakeholders may or may not be directly impacted by the technical changes, they will be acutely aware of how the change program could impact the business financially and their own reputations within the business and the market place. These two considerations make them a particularly important set of stakeholders. This is particularly true as you move towards the right. The change manager needs to work very closely with these stakeholders as they are not directly impacted by the change program, and can choose their own level of involvement.

This dual analysis is of critical importance when it comes to communicating with each stakeholder group. The primary stakeholders in the first analysis will need to be sold on how important the change program is to the business and how important they are to its success. At the other extreme are the priority stakeholders identified in the second analysis. As per the first group, these stakeholders will also need to be convinced that the change program is strategically important to the business. But they will also need to be convinced that the business improvement program is being well managed and that it is unlikely to have a detrimental impact on the reputation, operations or finances of the business. If any of these tests fail, then the program runs into the very real risk of being cancelled.

There is a further relationship between the two graphs. The senior stakeholders on the right will frequently have the organisational position and authority to instruct the stakeholders on the left. This makes these senior stakeholders even more important when it comes to designing the initial communications and prioritising which stakeholders need to be engaged with first.

There is one other stakeholder group that needs to be considered as part of the impact analysis, namely the business improvement team.

This is the group of people who are working full-time or close to it on delivering the business improvement project. They may or may not be part of the program office and frequently this team will be a blend of full-time employees and contractor staff.

For me, this is one of the most important stakeholder groups on the project. This team is a catalyst for change in the sense that they create change, but are not themselves changed. They are also a temporary group, constituted for the life of the program. For these reasons, they are seldom, if ever, evaluated as part of the impact study.

A key responsibility of this team is executing an effective communications strategy. They will decide on what messaging is communicated to which stakeholder group, on what frequency and format. The importance of getting this strategy right cannot be underestimated as it will directly influence how the business perceives the change program.

It is therefore vital that the health and competence of the team is measured and managed. If this team becomes disillusioned or suffers from poor morale, the consequences for the success of the program would be significant. Equally if this team does not have a common understanding of the objectives of the program or how the various projects fit together, then they will be prone to delivering mixed messages to the business and undermining the very change they are trying to create.

Stakeholder Communications

Two of the most substantial change programs I have been fortunate enough to work on over the course of my career couldn't have been more different from each other. In both cases, the organisation was a multi-billion-dollar company and the scope of each was multinational business transformation. Both programs impacted many thousands of workers and both comprised a suite of projects, each a substantial piece of work in its own right. Both programs were business critical and could bring down the company if they failed.

The first program was substantially more successful than the second.

There are many factors that could be blamed for the comparative failure of the second but, in my opinion, the biggest single cause of the failure was the inability of the program to communicate with the business. This meant that those involved in the day-to-day business did not understand what they needed to do and they got on with their day-to-day work. When they were asked to contribute, their effort was minimal. They did what they were asked and then they went back to work. To get anything done, the program office had to "push" the change into the business. There was no "pull" from the business to embed and own the change.

By comparison, the first program aggressively drove a well-structured communications strategy into the business that gave stakeholders predictability. Predictability of what was going to change, when, and why. When people have the information they need, they are more likely to act in a predictable way and are more likely to be accepting of the outcome, even if it is perceived as negative to them.

Both programs employed traditional communication activities such as town-hall meetings, presentations, email blasts, and monthly newsletters. Equally, both programs employed a group of change champions to represent the program, but with stark differences.

The first program engaged, trained, and deployed a very small group of change champions from the start of the program.

The second program established a very large group of change champions (over one hundred) and only mobilised them two thirds of the way through the program. Joining the program so late meant it was impossible for the change champions to fully grasp the complexity of the project and, as a result, they could not talk fluently about the program. This meant that they had to rely on presentation packs and written prompts. This ensured the delivery of the message was wooden and unengaging. Frequently, they were not able to provide the audience with any further information than what the audience already had. The number of change champions was also an issue. There were so many that they tended to leave it up to each other to communicate with the stakeholders. Naturally, this did not work.

In the first program, the change champion group was purposely designed to be far too small to be able to adequately provide the coverage the program required. Consequently, the change champions were forced to use the stakeholder groups to further promote the message. To this end, the program adopted a leverage model based on a ratio of 1:50.

Every change manager spoke to 50 stakeholders. Those 50 stakeholders spoke to 50 staff. This meant that the 10 change champions spoke to 500 stakeholders who spoke to 25000 staff. This strategy was key in forcing the stakeholders to engage in what was happening. Without their help, the project would fail. The business knew that.

The first program understood that stakeholders generally tend to remain distant and somewhat isolated from the program. To mitigate this issue, every communication included a call to action. The call to action answered the "so what?" questions: Why did you send me the communication? Why should I care, and most importantly, what do you want me to do? The call to action was tailored to the audience. By comparison, the second program adopted a simple communications plan, delivered on a "one shoe fits all" approach in the form of a regular monthly news update that failed to answer the "so what?" questions. Consequently, it completely failed to ask the stakeholders to do anything. There was no call to action and therefore, no action from the business.

Having an effective group of change champions is critical to the success of a change program, but having change champions is not enough. They need to be supported by a highly structured suite of communication activities including:

- One-to-one presentations
- One-to-few presentations
- One-to-many presentations
- Email
- Town-hall meetings
- Theatre
- Website updates
- Intranet forums
- Awareness education
- Workshops
- Technical training
- Posters, brochures, etc.

The delivery of these activities cannot be left to chance. To maximise success, a carefully thought through communications calendar is required. The communications calendar is the tool that establishes the rhythm of conversation between the business and the program office. It ensures that a cohesive suite of messages is sent out to the organisation on a predetermined frequency. It provides the foundation for predictability and dictates what type of message will go out on which day, to which audience, and in what format. In this way, the audience is trained to expect a communication on a given day and agree to take specific actions to support and promote the message to their nominated stakeholders.

In the following example of a change calendar, it can be seen that days 3, 4, and 5 are used to update the senior management group in the organisation. This is done in advance of a general email update which would go out on day 8. The internal newspaper is published on day 12. Up to now, communication has largely been one way. Days 15, 17, and 19 are then set aside for the organisation to ask questions directly to the program office and selected managers. The last week has no communications to minimise the issue of over-communicating.

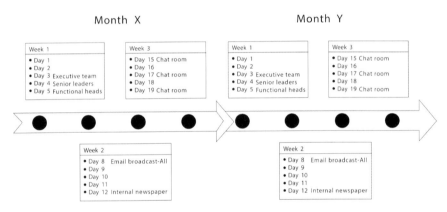

Establishing a communications rhythm seems simple and straightforward. But achieving this level of sophistication is not easy. First, you need agreement on who the stakeholders are. Then, you need to get those stakeholders to agree to listen to the message and, finally, you need to have their agreement that they will actively support and promote the message. This level of engagement is not achieved by email. If you send an email to a senior executive, there is almost zero chance of them reading it, and even less chance of them taking action as a result of it. But if you show up in their office and talk to them and brief them, they will listen and take action as needed. But to keep the stakeholders engaged, the message needs to continue to evolve. More of the same, or irrelevant information, will quickly turn stakeholders off. This brings us back to the final key difference between the two programs.

The first program completed an effective impact analysis. This resulted in agreement on how the stakeholders would be impacted by the various projects and how the stakeholders could influence the success of the program with their action or inaction, as the case may be.

The second program did not complete an impact analysis and it was left up to the various projects to work amongst themselves to determine the impacted stakeholders and the best way to engage them. This meant that key stakeholder groups were omitted and other stakeholders were engaged multiple times as each project reached out to them. This led to increased levels of confusion and irritation as the stakeholders did not receive a cohesive message.

A well-thought-out impact analysis will tell you what is going to happen when. The analysis typically works on the big picture and describes the project in chunks. The fine detail is seldom known in advance and senior stakeholders are not generally interested in the fine detail. It will be worked out later.

The impact analysis is then married to the change calendar. Now the change champions have something to discuss with the stakeholders. These communications should adopt the traditional model of last period, this period, next period. In this way, the change champion can review what has happened and discuss the success and failure of recent activities with the stakeholders. The stakeholder can be encouraged to support the bedding down of recent project activities, to create an environment where the program office is receiving meaningful feedback. The same applies to the current period. It is a discussion on what is currently happening, why it is happening, and what it means to the stakeholder. It is the time when the change champion can ask for the active support of the stakeholder for current activities. Finally, it is an opportunity to tell the stakeholder what to expect in the near and medium term and what will be expected of them in the future. The concept is illustrated overleaf.

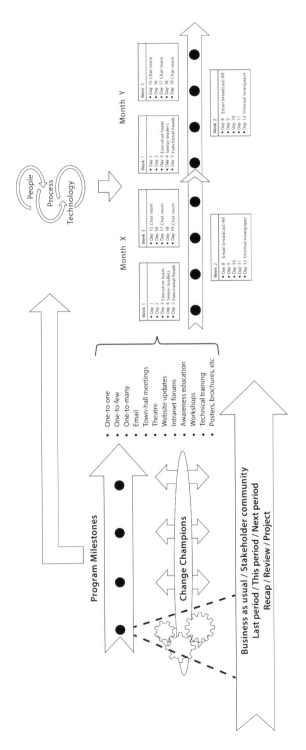

Irrespective of the volume, nature, and professionalism of delivery of the communications plan, stakeholders are going to say, "No one told me." A close cousin to this is the change manager who strenuously argues, "But I told them." These two scenarios cannot be avoided without active management.

The final piece of the communications puzzle: keeping track of who heard what, and when.

The first program used a common off-the-shelf content management system to track communications. Detailed stakeholder lists were created and the program kept track of which stakeholder saw which presentation and who presented it. Questions raised at these presentations were also tracked. Tracking was extended to include email broadcasts and attendance at online forums.

This detailed level of tracking reinforced to the stakeholders and the change champions that the communications were important and necessary. It kept them front of mind for all. It also improved attendance at all meetings and forums and increased the "read rate" of emails.

By contrast, the second program did not track communications and, as the go-live date drew close, the stakeholders took every opportunity to say, "But nobody told me" and "That won't work." Faced with a significant resistance to change, the program was forced to delay.

For communications to work, it is mandatory that there is consistency of the message across all channels. Communications that come from multiple authors are extremely distracting to the reader and it is impossible to harmonise the message. Having a single author ensures the look, style, and language are consistent throughout the messaging. Winston Churchill said, "If you have an important point to make, don't try to be subtle or clever. Use a pile driver. Hit the point once. Then come back and hit it again. Then hit it a third time—a tremendous whack."

On big projects it is difficult to achieve this, as it is frequently left up to the project managers to write their own communications. They also tend to have discretion on when they will communicate with the stakeholders. I consider both situations to be poor practice. Better practice is that the change manager owns the communications. They can work with a specialist writer as required, but this person must work for the change manager. The change manager should work with the project teams to develop a master slide pack. This pack will develop and grow over the course of the project. For each communication period in the communications calendar, the message will be drawn from this slide pack. Certain slides will be constant in every presentation, reinforcing the primary drivers of the program. These will be supported by new program information. Email broadcasts will reflect exactly the same information as will steering committee updates. Consistency creates momentum and momentum creates change.

The difference between the two programs highlights the fact that effective communication is not an art. It is a management discipline. If a business wants a change program to be effective, then there is no substitute for a consistent, integrated, carefully prepared and executed communications plan. After all, as Voltaire said, "To hold a pen is to be at war."

Stakeholder Messaging Strategy

Best practice states that before you begin a business improvement program you will have a detailed business case that clearly describes the endgame and what is required to get there.

The importance of being clear on the endgame cannot be overstated as it provides the bedrock for a successful change program. It becomes the foundation for all messaging and provides the criteria against which the change program is shaped, delivered, and measured. It also defines the hand-over criteria to business as usual.

When there is a clear endgame in place, the role of a change program is simply to establish a schedule of work that will deliver the endgame whilst bringing the organisation along on the journey.

Sounds straightforward, but in practice it is incredibly difficult. A core component to getting this right is ensuring there is alignment and consistency of message across all channels. This is a "must" from day zero of the program. Experience shows that there is a direct correlation between the number of stakeholders that agree on the endgame and the duration of the change program and, by extension, the size of the budget overrun. The lower the number, the bigger the budget overrun.

Getting the wider group of stakeholders to understand and support the endgame requires both a communications strategy and a separate messaging strategy. The communications strategy primarily describes the channels the change program will use to communicate with the stakeholders and the messaging strategy defines what the change program will tell them and when. While these two strategies go hand in hand, it is important that they are treated as different things. Blending them into one tends to be at the expense of the messaging strategy, whereas the messaging strategy should inform the communications strategy.

The biggest threat to the success of a business improvement program is stakeholder apathy. Getting the "business" to do something—make a decision, sign something off, host a get-together—is frequently very difficult. This is because, in the main, stakeholders are comfortable—they have their daily/weekly routines and habits and it is extremely difficult to get a stakeholder to change their behaviour. "Sure there is a change program on the go, but don't ask me to change. The business needs to change. I don't need to change." This is where the importance of getting the messaging right cannot be overstated.

Stakeholders forget that the business is only a collection of people working for a common purpose. The business doesn't behave. People behave. For the business to be different, people's behaviour needs to be different.

Effective messaging will assist each stakeholder to move through their own resistance to change and reach the key step of "Understanding" in the least amount of time.

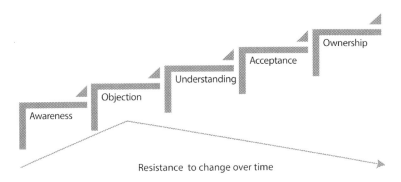

When a person starts to understand why things are as they are, then their objection to the proposed changes starts to decline and their acceptance of the new order grows. Eventually they take ownership of the change and become enlisted in the new direction.

To get stakeholders to be open to changing their behaviour, the change program needs to "turn up" either the "pleasure" or the "pain" threshold in the business. "Pleasure" means making the future look so attractive everybody wants it. "Pain" requires painting a very bleak future for the business if it doesn't change. Working in the middle of these two parameters is unlikely to yield much success.

Moving the organisation to either end requires understanding from the stakeholders. They need to get it. This is why effective messaging is so critical to the success of the change program. Achieving a critical mass of understanding requires actively talking to the stakeholders in their language. For the best effect, the change program needs to treat the messaging strategy as a propaganda program. All communications need to hang together and they need to be aligned to the endgame. The objective is to cause many people to all see things the same way and for them to become willing to adjust their behaviour as required. Relying on individual project managers to choose what to say about their part of the program, and when to say it, substantially increases the likelihood of leaving the stakeholders under or misinformed about the program.

The following table is a practical means of capturing the high-level messaging strategy. Using broad language, it maps the current behaviour by stakeholder group to the required behaviour and the associated messaging.

The table assumes the change program is an acquisition. The company is being bought. The concept is illustrated overleaf.

Stakeholder	Current behaviour	Program Stage			Key messages in	Key messages out
		Start Up	Growth	Operate		
Stakeholder group 1 Example: Senior Executive Team.	• Decision makers. • Monthly business review meetings. • Removed from daily operations. • Working behind the scenes.	• Highly visible. • Promote the program. • Walk the talk. • Introduce KPI's on direct reports to measure engagement in the change program. • Implement an out of cycle review meeting specifically for making decisions for the change program.	• Highly visible. • Promote the program. • Walk the talk. • Actively manage variances for direct reports engagement with and in the change program. • Increase KPI set to include 'operate' PKI's for new mode of operations. • Update position descriptions for senior managers.	• Promote the program. • Walk the talk.	• This acquisition needs your active support. • Your behaviour and words will measurably impact the success of the acquisition. • The change program is not being done within the company - it is being done to it. • Your role is to minimise the shock of the changes. **Call to action** • You need to change your behaviour. • You need to be seen in the business.	• It would be irresponsible of us to resist the acquisition. • The acquisition is a good strategy for this organisation. • We have too much at stake to resist this acquisition. • We have a sense of duty to work toward this program. • We think that our organisation will benefit from this acquisition. • The acquisition matches the priorities of our organisation. • This acquisition will improve our organisation's overall efficiency. • We believe in the acquisition. • It would be too costly for us to resist the change. **Call to action** • When called on please participate honestly and openly. • If you have concerns tell us.
Stakeholder group 2					• Without your active support the acquisition will be undermined.. • We respect the load you are already carrying. You will need to carry an extra load. • You are now the face of the change program. • You need to always be positive in your messages to the business. **Call to action** • Promote the program in every meeting. • Allow staff to express concerns. • If you don't have answer talk to the change team.	

The key take out from the table is that the messages used to sell the project are expected to be different by stakeholder group, but the outbound message, for all stakeholder groups to use when discussing the change program, needs to be consistent.

Consider political parties running for elections. The last thing they need is to confuse the electorate, and on a daily basis the party will issue talking points. This ensures that each politician says essentially the same thing, but from the angle of their portfolio. It doesn't matter what question they are asked. The politician will trot out some verbiage that bridges from the question to the talking points and then repeats the talking points.

I am not suggesting that the change program adopt the same level of deflection as politicians. But the principle is sound. The change manager needs to work with the stakeholders to ensure they all use the same phrases and messages when describing the change program. As the program matures, the phrases will change and evolve to reflect the new status.

There is a reference to "call to action" in the table. It is there to ensure that the call to action is not forgotten. The call to action is the specific things the change program requires from the stakeholder. It's remarkable how many communications I see that seek action from the stakeholders or wider community, without actually asking for it. And then the change agent complains that they are being ignored.

It is expected that the call to action will be designed to deliver the desired behavioural changes from each stakeholder group. An effective filter for evaluating a message is to ask, "So what? What do I want the reader/participant to do as a result of receiving the message? Does the message ask them to do that?" In my view, there is always a call to action. Sometimes the action will be quite passive such as the classic "keep calm and carry on." At other times, it will be a request for active participation such as "log in and check your details." Always indicate to the stakeholder whether the message requires "noting," "a decision," or "discussion." This will help define the call to action.

It is relatively straightforward to establish effective communication channels between the change program and the business, but it is incredibly difficult to get stakeholders to understand what is meant by a specific message. It is remarkable how people will interpret what was supposed to be a straightforward communication.

What you heard is not what I said, and

What I said is not what I want and

What I want is not what I need.

> Same time next week then...

The average stakeholder in a large business is a highly competent professional manager, but when it comes to change they are at best, a part-timer. This means that they speak a different language, see the world through different frameworks, and have a completely different set of priorities when it comes to what's important for the business. By different language, I mean that manufacturing staff speak Manufacturing, IT staff speak IT, finance staff speak Finance and change practitioners speak the language of Change. It is incumbent on the change practitioner to learn the languages of the stakeholders and talk to them in those languages.

A different language is a different vision of life. Federico Fellini

For example, when discussing the change program with the financial manager, framing the benefits in terms of how the balance sheet will be improved and which items in the profit and loss statement will be impacted, will likely hold their attention. India uses a different scale when it comes to currency. Indians are comfortable with lakh and crore and Europeans are comfortable with thousands and millions. Two people could be saying exactly the same thing, both speaking English, but in a different language when it comes to numbers. It would not help much if the numbers were written down, as the comma is placed differently in each scale. Without careful attention to detail, a misunderstanding on which are the important numbers could be created very quickly.

I note that one of the most important communication channels, and one that is frequently undervalued, is the hierarchy of meetings within an organisation. There is no one better to put the change message in context for their subordinates than their manager. As noted, a manufacturing manager will speak in manufacturing terms and examples.

It doesn't matter who the audience is, when it comes to messaging, there are a few universal rules that apply.

- Value is more important than cost. Going cheap is more likely to damage the image of the change program and could cost substantially more in the long run.
- Use graphs, charts, tables, and diagrams. "A picture is worth a thousand words."
- Be succinct. Use short sharp sentences. This takes time and effort. It is not practical to prepare communications at the last moment. In the words of Mark Twain: "I didn't have time to write a short letter, so I wrote a long one instead."
- Repetition works. Use repetition in the same communication and across multiple communications and channels.
- Write to the individual, not the group.
- Use sentences or words that indicate willingness by the change program to engage in a larger dialogue with the stakeholders.
- Select the right channel. Just because there are many communication channels available to the change program does not mean the program needs to use them all, all the time. Blanketing stakeholders with messages can be counterproductive. They just turn off.
- Exposure does not equal engagement. Just because a million people might watch a show on TV doesn't mean that the same million people will watch the advertising at halftime. Or in business terms, just because the change program does an email blast, or publishes a newspaper, does not mean the communication will be read.

In summary, write in a way that makes stakeholders want to engage with the message and want to participate in the change program. Stakeholders will naturally spread a message that resonates with them, and just as quickly ignore those that don't.

As a tail piece to this article, the following is a simple framework that helps to ensure the channel strategy and message strategy are kept separate, but remain related. The key is working out the message summary. Once you know what you want to say per program phase, it becomes easier to complete the rest of the framework. The framework can be modified to suit your needs. The concept is illustrated overleaf.

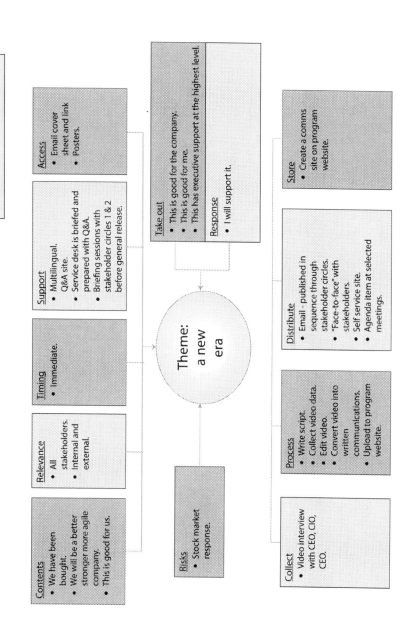

Program phase - Start Up

Message summary
- We have been bought.
- We believe in the acquisition.
- This is good for us.

Contents
- We have been bought.
- We will be a better stronger more agile company.
- This is good for us.

Relevance
- All stakeholders.
- Internal and external.

Timing
- Immediate.

Support
- Multilingual.
- Q&A site.
- Service desk is briefed and prepared with Q&A.
- Briefing sessions with stakeholder circles 1 & 2 before general release.

Access
- Email cover sheet and link
- Posters.

Take out
- This is good for the company.
- This is good for me.
- This has executive support at the highest level.

Response
- I will support it.

Theme: a new era

Risks
- Stock market response.

Collect
- Video interview with CEO, CIO, CEO.

Process
- Write script.
- Collect video data.
- Edit video.
- Convert video into written communications.
- Upload to program website.

Distribute
- Email - published in sequence through stakeholder circles.
- "Face-to-face" with stakeholders.
- Self service site.
- Agenda item at selected meetings.

Store
- Create a comms site on program website.

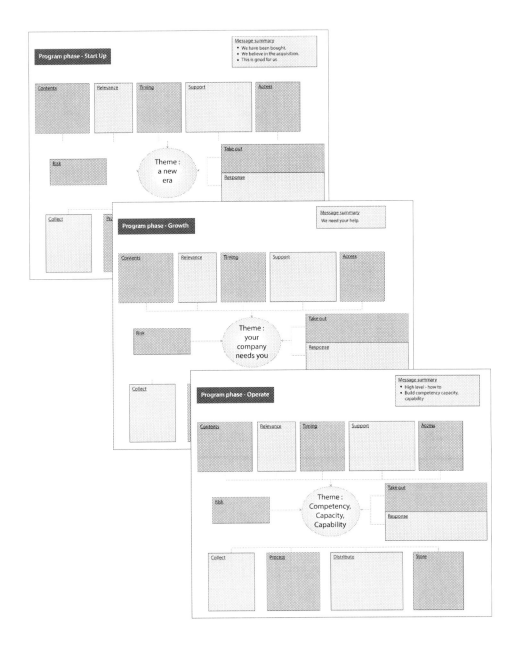

Invariably, change programs are sold with three word slogans such as "Transition, Transform, Extend" or "Stabilise, Consolidate, Transform" or similar. The previous graphic shows how this principle is used with the above framework.

The reference to risk is important. It captures risks such as getting the message wrong, the message going public, what happens if the message is misinterpreted, and what happens if the message is not received at all. The author always knows what they intended to say. Asking a third party to review the message in a cold reading will quickly determine whether what was intended to be the message is the actual message conveyed.

What you heard is not what I said, and

What I said is not what I want and

What I want is not what I need.

Same time next week then...

In a holistic approach, the risks should be in the risk register and have mitigations associated with them. The channel strategy should then be refined to help mitigate the risk. For example, some messages are best delivered verbally to ensure a document cannot be leaked to the press. Other documents could be delivered to a restricted audience with a caution for confidentiality.

Measuring Stakeholder Engagement

In any business transformation program, there are three primary stakeholder groups: the change team, the business leadership team, and everyone else. The change team is the group of people who work in the change program on behalf of the business. The other two groups represent the business. The difference between the two is defined as those who commission and lead change and those that receive or follow change. For the purposes of this article I will refer to them as leaders and followers respectively, and collectively they are referred to as the business.

I am a strong believer in the principle that the change team cannot change the business. Only the business can change the business. The change team works on behalf of the business. If the business does not want to change, then there is little the change team can do about it.

Simply put, the change team may be responsible for day-to-day change activities, but the business is never absolved of its accountability for the success of the change program.

It is reasonable to say that the central tenet of the change agents' mandate is to ensure the organisation successfully moves through the business improvement journey with the least amount of disruption to the operations as possible. Or in other words, the mandate is to reduce the depth and width of the change curve.

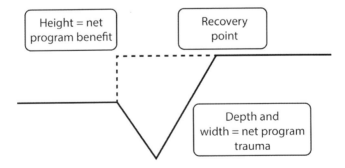

Typically the change manager will administer a periodic stakeholder engagement survey to predict and evaluate how successfully the business is transitioning across the change curve. Key to achieving success is that the business acknowledges and accepts its accountability for the quality of the deliverables arising from the change program and for ensuring the benefits are realised and sustainable.

Predicting future success requires understanding the past. If the survey identifies what has not worked "so far," then it is reasonably easy to extrapolate what will or won't work in the future.

The problem is that the surveys don't pick up the issues early enough. This is because they typically ask the same questions of all stakeholders to support a "compare and contrast" analysis across the organisation. This approach will not provide a complete or relevant picture. That requires the survey to recognise the difference between leaders and followers and to ask questions relevant to each group.

In any organisation, there are only a handful of senior managers with sufficient authority to make decisions that will cause material changes to the business and without doubt, the biggest killer of success for any change program is the inability of the change team to get these leaders to make a decision.

The reasons for not making a decision are varied and include:

1. The decision-maker does not actually have the authority to make the decision, and won't admit it.
2. The decision-maker does not understand the change program and therefore does not understand the consequences of making or not making a decision.
3. The decision-maker does not have the confidence to make a decision.
4. The decision requires the approval/endorsement of a committee.

The first three are particularly disruptive. When a manager acts as if they have authority to make decisions and they do not, they destroy the change program's momentum as it tables decision after decision and nothing happens. This includes the situation where senior management has specifically inserted a manager into the change program without giving them the authority or support to make necessary decisions. At best, a manager like that is a post box who relays messages to senior management. At worst, they can cause the program to fail.

The decision-maker that does not understand the change program is not only disruptive, but also dangerous. It is not necessarily a case of the manager being lazy or disinterested. It may just be that the manager is so busy with their day-to-day activities that they leave the change program to do its own thing. The consequence is that they will not be close enough to the program to appreciate the impact of making or not making the decision. As an example, the manager may decide to extend the delivery date on a change program without realising that it will cause the company to miss key dates in its audit schedule. This may invalidate the insurance cover and leave the company seriously exposed.

These problems are amplified when a committee is involved and especially when the committee meets on a fixed schedule. Any decision that is not taken in one meeting, is held over to the next, or the one following that. These delays can have a significant knock-on effect on the change program.

The leaders' engagement survey needs to identify if these types of issues exist. Or in other words, do the leaders accept their accountability for the quality of the deliverables arising from the change program and for ensuring the benefits are realised and sustainable?

The survey questions could be as follows. These questions are not intended to be exhaustive.

Accountability

"Being personally accountable for your actions and omissions." This presupposes the ability to accept the responsibility to carry out assigned tasks and having sufficient authority to carry them out.

- Do you fully understand the impact your position can have on the success of the change program?
- Have you been asked to make a formal decision?
- Have you been asked to make a decision outside of your delegated authority?

- Have you followed up to determine if any decision you have taken is being followed?
- Have you requested an impact statement to understand the impact of decisions you deferred?
- Are your colleagues aware of the decisions you have made?
- Are you aware of decisions your colleagues have deferred?
- Have you or your colleagues changed your behaviour as a result of a decision you have taken?
- Do you have value to add, but lack the forum to add it?

Quality

Working to agreed standards. This requires that the manager is appropriately educated to be able to take responsibility for their actions. It also places responsibility on the manager to maintain their competence by continuing to educate themselves about the deliverables while working within appropriate bounds.

- Can you describe what the change program deliverable will look like in your area?
- Can you describe what you will do differently as a result of the change program?
- Can you describe what your staff will do differently as a result of the change program?
- What have you done to satisfy yourself that the deliverables will be fit for purpose?
- Do you attend a regular briefing on the change program?
- Have you posed any questions to the change program on the nature of the deliverables?
- Have you requested further information from the change program?

Sustainability

Deliverables need to be adequate for present needs as well as developing capacity to meet future requirements.

- Can you clearly describe how you will measure the success of the program?

- Can you describe what formal actions you are taking today to make sure the change program is successful today and in the future?
- Do you actively hold your colleagues to account for inadequate support of the change program?
- Are you implementing additional plans to address related and necessary actions that are out of scope to the change program?

When it comes to the follower group, the questions must necessarily be different to those of the leaders. Followers do not have the authority to make binding decisions on the company. But given the relative volume of this group, they do have the means to derail any change initiative. It is therefore equally important to measure and track the mood of this community.

When measuring the followers' engagement with the change program, the oft-heard phrase is "resistance to change." My experience is that a survey seldom, if ever, will identify resistance to change. This is not to say that resistance to change does not exist. Rather when it exists and is material, it is normally so obvious that a survey is not required. Examples could be unionised workplaces, or the resistance is from one highly influential person. This could be the CIO who is having a new IT system imposed on him by the CEO.

It is largely irrelevant if an individual is resistant to change as it is near impossible for the change team to manage change at the individual level. It is acknowledged that there will always be staff who are late adopters of change and it is acceptable to give them time to come around to the need for the change program. Managing these staff is the responsibility of the line manager.

One of the reasons I don't like the phrase "resistance to change" is that it is easier to brand someone as resistant to change than it is to take the time to find out why an individual or group appears hesitant/resistant to engage more fully with the change program. Just because they have concerns with the change program does not make them resistant to change. Frequently it is only a case that they do not feel ready for the change.

There is an enormous difference between readiness for change and resistance to change. It should be expected that staff will always question if they, or their organisation, is ready for the proposed changes to take effect. This does not mean that they are resisting change. Rather they are confirming for themselves whether the organisation is ready. Unfortunately, this type of hesitancy is frequently interpreted as resistance to change. The consequence is that any concerns staff have about organisational readiness are frequently met with practical indifference by the leadership. I use the phrase "practical indifference" as change programs will readily talk about the importance of measuring stakeholder engagement, but the majority don't do anything practical about it. They tend to adopt the view that followers should join in or "get off the bus."

There are two categories associated with readiness: personal readiness and organisational readiness. In this article, the term "readiness" refers to the human level. It excludes technical readiness such as installing technology of some sort.

While the two categories are only loosely related, organisational readiness should follow personal readiness, as sustainable business outcomes require that most stakeholders need to be neutral or better in their support for the change. Organisational change readiness then can be built on the back of this support.

In addition, the survey needs to reflect the phase of the program.

It is common for a change program to have multiple named phases such as "mobilise, analyse, and implement" or "stabilise, transform, and extend." The labels used will depend on the nature of the change program. Using the same set of questions for each phase would not evaluate the maturity expected from each phase. Asking a stakeholder if they have heard of the change program makes sense in phase 1, but offers little value in future phases. Conversely, by the time the program enters its final phase, it is critical that followers consider themselves competent and capable to operate in the new world.

While the questions should change between phases, it makes sense to use the same headers or categories across all phases. Example categories are Awareness, Acceptance, and Attitude for personal readiness and Alignment, Capability, Capacity, and Competency for organisational readiness.

Personal change readiness	Organisational change readiness
• **Awareness** - *the extent to which staff understand the nature of the change.*	• **Alignment** - *the extent to which staff understand how the change program aligns with the company mission and objectives.*
• **Acceptance** - *the extent to which staff accept the need for the organisation to change.*	• **Capability** - *the extent to which staff understand how the capabilities of the organisation will change as a result of the change program.*
• **Attitude** - *the extent to which staff have a personal desire for the change to be successful and are willing to assist as required.*	• **Competency** - *the extent to which staff understand the skill profile required to deliver the organisational capability.*
	• **Capacity** - *the extent to which staff understand how much of the new capability is required.*

The following table provides example of the concepts to be tested at each level of maturity.

	Program phase		
	Phase 1	Phase 2	Phase 3
Awareness	I know what the program is called.	I know what is expected of me.	I know what to do when the change is implemented.
Acceptance	I know why it is important.	The change program is a good strategy for this organisation.	I am excited about the furure.
Attitude	I want to support it.	It would be irresponsible not to support the change program.	I do not anticipate any problems adjusting to the work I will have when this program is adopted.
Alignment	I understand how the change program fits with the corporate strategy.	Our organisation's top decision-makers have put all their support behind this project effort.	My new KPIs are relevant to the new world
Capability		I know what the organisation wants to achieve.	I have the technology and tool I need to complete my day-to-day tasks after the program is implemented.
Competency		I know how the organisation s overall skills mix will need to change.	I am trained and ready for the future.
Capacity		I understand the productivity demands in the new model.	The change program will improve our organisation's overall efficiency.

I close with the observation that a survey does not fix issues and it only provides answers to the questions it asks.

A change program with strong leadership, that demands accountability from the leaders, will always deliver a solid result. You don't need a survey to tell you that.

Developing Human Capital

It's the difference between know how and know why. It's the difference between, say, being trained as a pilot to fly a plane and being educated as an aeronautical engineer and knowing why the plane flies, and then being able to improve its design so that it will fly better. Clearly both are necessary, so this is not putting down the Know-How person; if I am flying from here to there I want to be in the plane with a trained pilot (though if the pilot knows the Why as well, then all the better, particularly in an emergency).

The difference, also, is fundamentally that Know How is learning to Think Other People's Thoughts, which indeed is also the first stage in education—in contrast to learning to Think Your Own Thoughts, which is why Know Why is the final state of education. Indeed, both Know How and Know Why are essential at one moment or another, and they interact all the time; but at the same time, the centre of gravity of education is and must be in the Know Why.

The Phi Kappa Phi Journal, Spring 2000, p. 46. (author unknown).

......

Recently I was chatting with a colleague about some of the strangest things we had been involved in over the years as business consultants. I told him a story about the time I was asked to deliver education to a group of miners in Africa. The objective of the course was to improve their supervisory skills. What made the class interesting was that the miners spoke little or no English and I did not speak their language. Furthermore, the class was to take place about a kilometre underground in what could only be described as a cave. It had no electricity, no chairs, no tables, no flipchart, and no whiteboard. It was just a hole, in a hole, deep underground. The class had to be underground as the miners were only allowed a short time away from the working face.

To deliver the class, I prepared a storyboard on a large and long strip of brown paper, rolled it up, and went down the hole. In the cave I hung the storyboard with some wire I found hanging from the roof. When the participants came in, the only lights we had were the headlamps miners wear underground. This meant that for them to see the material they all had to switch on their lamps and stare at the storyboard. This actually provided a good way of knowing when their attention drifted, as they would turn away and the light would go out. I worked with an interpreter and we delivered a successful course.

The students had been identified as potential supervisors and the underground course was part of a program aimed at building the overall basket of skills they would need to become productive supervisors. The program was delivered in two phases. The first phase was education and focused on creating an awareness of the concepts and vocabulary typically employed by a supervisor. The second phase was training. The focus was experiential learning in a live environment; the active transfer of skills. To this end I spent hours working "on the floor" with each of the supervisors, supporting them individually as they learnt their new roles.

The outcome was that mutual respect between the miners and the new supervisors was quickly established. Collectively they soon became an effective team and the client received an excellent financial return.

For me, what made this project different is that it went against the norm. Frequently when staff are promoted from the floor to the supervisory or managerial positions, they are not educated or trained in how to operate in their new roles. This invariably means that the organisation loses a good worker and gains a poor supervisor. Educating and training the miners on how to supervise ensured that the mine not only gained a team of supervisors who had a first-hand understanding of the daily working environment faced by the staff, but also a team who understood what was required to effectively supervise the staff.

The experience really taught me that staff (human capital) should always be developed through a holistic program that combines education and active training. Education provides the framework and context. It explains why something is important—the sessions in the cave. Training develops technique, skills, and tactics as evidenced by working "on the floor" with the supervisors. The term "on the floor" means exactly that—working with the employees, including managers, in the live environment. Relying on generic training exercises in the classroom as a substitute for "on the floor" experience is a far cry from working with each student directly on the job as they actively learn to address real operational issues.

From a big picture point of view and as illustrated in the graphic, business objectives are delivered through the capabilities of the organisation. Capabilities are themselves created from a blend of the enablers of finance, technology, and the human capital.

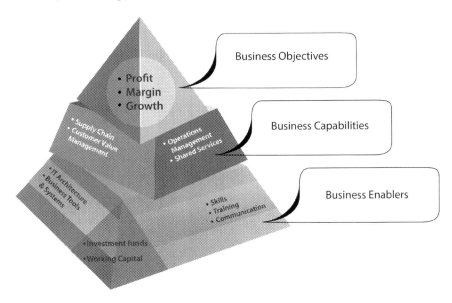

When it comes to building human capital there really is only one objective—to cause a change in behaviour. A change in behaviour means doing things differently because of new skills or because you see the world differently. When constructing a program to develop human capital, it is important to be clear on which business capabilities need to be created or augmented and how the new behaviours will support the business capabilities.

No matter whether the intent is a skill or a knowledge transfer, there is an important hierarchy that needs to be acknowledged—organisational learning "sits" above individual learning.

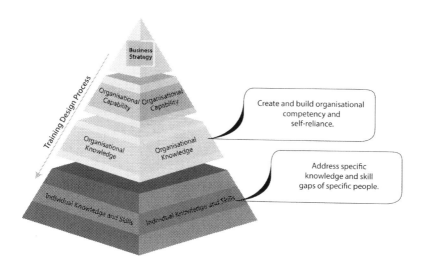

Equally important is the difference between the learning attributes of the organisation and those of the individual. Organisations can be educated, in the sense that they can have memory and retain knowledge. Organisations cannot be skilled. Individuals can be educated and skilled.

Acknowledging the hierarchy and the learning attributes of each part is vital as they directly inform which stakeholders need to be engaged as part of any human capital development program.

Consider the following scenario. As part of normal business practice, the sales and marketing team meets clients and receives orders which they then pass onto the production department. The production department translates the request into finished goods. The production manager seldom, if ever, meets the customer.

To keep up with best practice, the production department sends an engineer on a training course as a refresher on the latest production techniques. This is effectively a reskilling of the engineer.

It is easy to see how the separation of duties could result in the production department not considering it relevant to inform the sales and marketing team of the engineer's refresher training.

If the sales and marketing team does not know that the engineer has an increased skill set, they will not change what they sell or how they sell it and the business will not make a meaningful return on its investment in the engineer's development.

To mitigate this risk, the process of arranging training for the engineer should include an organisational education component to drive organisational learning.

This raises the question—which stakeholders need to be educated to meet any given organisational learning objective? The following table can assist.

	Impacted Stakeholders		Business Impact	
Capability	Direct	Indirect	Customer	Financial

The impacted stakeholder columns capture which functions are directly and indirectly responsible for ensuring the business capability is created. The difference between the two is critical in that indirect stakeholders rely on the direct stakeholders to inform them of newly created capabilities and direct stakeholders rely on the indirect stakeholders to maximise the potential created by the enhanced capability.

In the above example, the production function is the directly impacted stakeholder and the sales and marketing team is the indirectly impacted stakeholder. Other indirect stakeholders could include the up and down stream functions in the value chain.

When it comes to realising a return on investment from the capabilities created by a human development program, perhaps the most important development activity is educating the business that the new capability exists.

Allied to this is the following key question. Is the direct stakeholder equipped to manage the up- skilled resource? All too frequently after a development program, I have heard managers telling their staff words to the effect of "this is the real world" and they "should forget that academic mumbo-jumbo and get on with the job." Simply put, for the business to fully realise the benefits of the development program, it may be necessary to require the manager to attend a course on management techniques.

This highlights the importance of the business impact columns.

Frequently courses are measured in terms of attendance and student satisfaction. These are good measures of benefits to the students themselves, but they tell you nothing about the effectiveness of the course itself. The true benefit of the program should be measured through changes in key business indicators such as revenue, margins, yield, utilisation, productivity, quality, and scrap. Linking the measurement of course effectiveness to key business indicators requires a much deeper understanding of the impacted stakeholder community. This requires an understanding of the corporate scorecard and, by extension, the wider stakeholder (direct and indirect) community.

As discussed previously, a development program must align the learning outcomes to the business objectives, thereby providing context for the sessions.

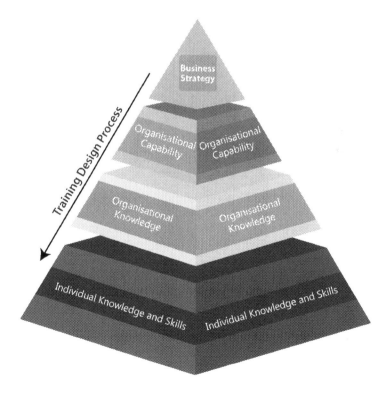

I recommend using the following table.

Objective	Capability	Course	Description	Module	Module Description	Learning Outcomes		
						Skills Developed	Knowledge Gained	Behavioural Changes Sought

The first two columns provide the context for the human capital development program and collectively they link the course outcomes to the business capabilities.

It is one thing to know why and what you need to do and another thing to know how to do it. This gap exists because while knowledge can be retained at the organisation or team level, skill can only be captured at the individual level. The problem is that individuals leave, taking their skills with them.

To mitigate this, all human capital development programs should include a component that will actively contribute towards infusing the organisation with knowledge, thus reducing the reliance on a specific individual. This reinforces why Organisational Knowledge sits above Individual Knowledge and Skill in the hierarchy.

Focusing on three different learning outcomes will ensure this happens.

Learning Outcomes		
Skills Developed	Knowledge Gained	Behavioural Changes Sought

The first column defines the specific skills an individual will acquire. The second column defines the knowledge the organisation can expect to gain because of the skills improvement program. It should include knowledge gained by direct and indirect stakeholders. If there is no skills development program, then column two will be completed accordingly.

Column three is the most critical aspect of the entire development program. In many respects, it is the sum of columns one and two. Correctly completed, it will bring together, all the threads discussed in this article. It:

- Describes the tangible differences expected from the program and will inform columns one and two.
- Answers the question—how differently does the organisation need to behave for it to benefit from the investment in columns one and two? It should be tied to the business benefits.
- Reinforces the universal point that no matter what the improvement initiative is, it will require an understanding of the wider stakeholder group and their interests

Cross-Border Stakeholder Management (the Last 5 Percent)

Recently I was walking in Patna, the main city of Bihar, India, on my way to a meeting with a departmental secretary in the state government. I walked on the side of the road, against the flow of traffic. And just because I was walking against the traffic did not mean I had only to watch out for oncoming traffic. Far from it. I had a reasonable chance of being run over from behind as cars and motorbikes frequently drove the wrong way up the road. Day-to-day life was definitely different to what I knew from living in Australia.

Having spent a year in Bihar, I had come to feel at home in India. I found India similar to South Africa, the country I grew up in. Both countries have a "can-do, make-do" attitude, and people are allowed to do their own thing. If you get hurt or killed because you're being stupid, then that is on you and you don't get to sue everybody that you can think of. Australia is different. It is a world where the government tries to legislate safety into every facet of life. Folks are often heard referring to Australia as a nanny state or a nation of headmasters. This quality does not make Australia an unpleasant place to live. On the contrary, it is a very safe country with a great social safety net. A calm, well-structured, predictable society.

And importantly, for me, Australia represented "normal." It was my yardstick.

Somewhere along my walk I realised that Australia was the odd one out. Australia does not represent normal. If anything, it represents abnormal. It belongs to a minority group of countries, each of which has an advanced social and physical infrastructure. A common characteristic of these countries is that day-to-day life is stable and predictable. Stability provides a secure platform for business and allows change and business managers the luxury of worrying about the smaller things—the cohesiveness of a stakeholder message, the quality of a PowerPoint pack, dress codes, whether staff should take the train or a cab to the airport when travelling, and if staff crossed at the traffic lights in accordance with the safety policy. Or in other words—the last 5 percent.

As an example, working in Australia, I was critiqued in my role as a change manager because a senior stakeholder was given the same briefing from two different change champions. Ideally, you don't want this to happen, but in the greater scheme of things it is a small issue, a first world problem— the last 5 percent.

By comparison, countries like India are in the majority. These countries are still wrestling with how to develop the basics of their social and physical infrastructures. They are characterised by inadequate sanitation, limited access to clean water, poor heating, questionable health services, excessive bureaucracy, corruption, and an inefficient legal system. For the sake of a label, I term these countries the first 50 percent. For countries in the first 50 percent, day-to-day life is neither predictable nor stable. A bus trip to work could take one hour or six hours. There is no way to know except to take the bus and find out. When you cannot rely on the social and physical infrastructure, you live with a high degree of uncertainty. In Australia, I could travel for business, confident in the knowledge that if a family member needed emergency medical treatment, it would be readily available. The infrastructure would mobilise and my family would receive excellent medical attention. In the first 50 percent, this support is not readily available. Families rely on each other, and in an emergency, it is the family that must immediately respond. It could have disastrous consequences to leave the emergency in the hands of the social infrastructure.

I re-examined the following question, one I had been asked twice in my consulting career. How would you deal with cultural differences with respect to stakeholder management on an international business improvement program? In each case, my answer was strong enough for me to get the role, but with hindsight, I recognise that the question and my answer were both off-target. The question should have been this one. Using the simple definition of culture as "the way we do things around here" and applying it at a state or country level, how would you deal with the operational differences arising in each country as they impact the transformation program?

This wider definition recognises that "the way we do things around here" is largely defined by the (un)predictability of the social and physical infrastructure and that consequential business operating models cater for the degree in variability in either the last 5 percent or the first 50 percent.

What this means for cross-border stakeholder management is that the standard issues of cultural awareness such as presenting a business card with two hands, whether you sit women next to men, whether you wear a head scarf or hat, or if you use formal titles for people you know well, are of lesser concern. What is more important is to understand and respond to how things operate in each market—the physical aspect of "the way we do things around here."

Any consideration that individuals from the first 50 percent cannot perform at the highest levels expected by the last 5 percent is completely unwarranted. That notion is fully debunked by the performance of almost every person who has physically moved to a last 5 percent working environment. Equally, the impact of the local constraints is often evidenced when a last 5 percent manager moves to a first 50 percent market and is unable to perform at the same level as they achieved in the first 5 percent market.

Consider, two countries, two companies. For the sake of the discussion, country A represents a last 5 percent company and country B, a first 50 percent company.

Country A, Company A   Country B, Company B

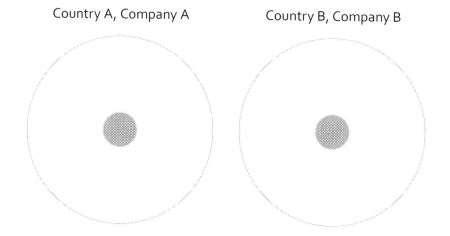

The companies are part of a market. Each market has its own culture and each company works effectively within that market. For me, the markets are loosely characterised as follows:

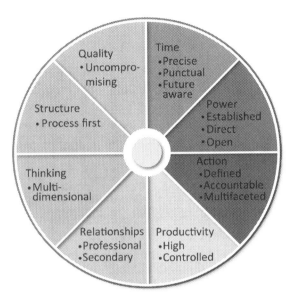

Last 5 percent

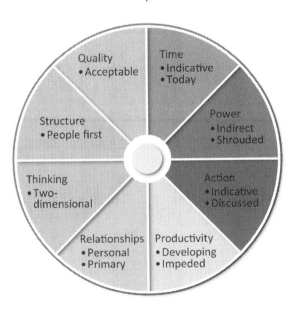

First 50 percent

These cultural norms are reinforced as each company interacts with other companies in the market. I define "market" as any business community working with the same constraints as your own.

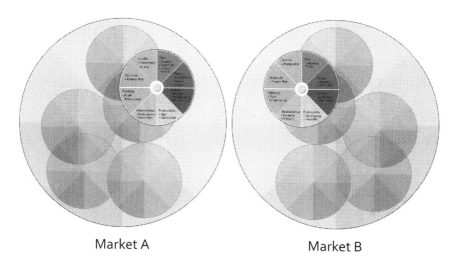

Market A   Market B

Each company understands the rules of the local market and the constraints of the local operating environment. This includes tender processes, logistics, payment terms, corruption, and what is generally acceptable behaviour.

The two markets work well when independent of each other. Issues only arise when the two environments are forced to operate as if they were the same business, as is often the case when a company outsources a business function.

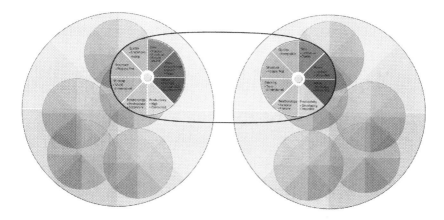

In this example, company B is contracted to act as if it is company A. Staff based in the last 50 percent are expected to think and behave as if they are working and living in a last 5 percent country. This expectation is unrealistic. How does a person who deals with two or three power failures a year understand a person working in an environment where they can be a daily occurrence? Can a person who has only ever lived in the last 5 percent understand the priorities of a person who may work in a modern city, but has an ancestral home that has no running water or flush toilets? How does a first 50 percent person understand why a last 5 percent person gets upset because the closest printer to them is not working?

Differences in the social and operational infrastructure in each country have a material impact on how easily staff engage with the nuances of a business improvement project. It is easy to understand why a person who has just caught three buses to work because (once again) their train never showed up, or (once again) they had no breakfast because their water tank failed to fill overnight or because their suburb was (once again) hit with a rolling blackout, would be less concerned with a conversation on whether a manager should have seven or eight direct reports. You can hear them screaming—let's deal with real issues.

The most significant consequence of working with either an advanced or developing physical and social infrastructure is how each community respects time. The last 5 percent are driven by time. Meetings are expected to start on time; action plans are agreed with an anticipation that the actions will be executed as agreed. Month-end runs to a schedule and the quarterly reporting cycle is predictable. Conversely, the last 50 percent do not hold time in such high esteem. It is not because they don't want to, but rather because, as much as they might want to be punctual, business has learnt that the inadequacies of the infrastructure mean that life is not always predictable. A phrase frequently heard in India is that IST, Indian standard time, actually means "Indian stretchable time," as a disparaging comment on the frequent lack of punctuality. Other examples include, "there is no rush in Africa," or "it's Island time." For these markets, there is always a negative impact on productivity.

For a program manager, having a team that has a degree of indifference to the clock is frightening. The most basic requirement for effective stakeholder management is:

Do what you say you will do, when you said you would do it.

In other words, be reliable and consistent.

When a change program loses faith in time, then everything begins to drift. When the senior stakeholder group loses confidence in the business improvement team's ability to manage to schedule, the change program loses credibility.

The interview question remains unanswered. How do you manage stakeholders when working with or in the first 50 percent?

A better answer to the question would be that the first 5 percent should take the time to build relationships based on trust, respect, and a firsthand understanding of the local conditions.

I am quite confident that any program manager would quickly argue that they are a team player and that they respect relationships. I am not talking about being extra polite to each other, or having a sharing session at the start of a workshop. Rather, I am talking about taking one or two months to build a team that fully understands the constraints and pressures experienced in each market and then resource the team appropriately. The phrase "walk in their shoes" is highly relevant. It takes time to understand the local market.

The last 5 percent tend to treat everyone equally and adopt a highly professional approach to business, as in, "You don't have to be my friend, just do your job." This approach works well when working within the same market, but is unlikely to work with the first 50 percent.

For the first 50 percent, strong relationships are the glue that holds everything together as the operational difficulties ebb and flow. When you can't rely on the local infrastructure then all you have left are relationships. Strong relationships build the confidence to rely on each other to help as needed. To go the extra mile when time slips.

My recommendation is that the program manager rents an apartment in the local city for a month and lives as a local. This will earn the respect of the local team and establish insights that cannot be gained from the safe cocoon of a hotel. A firsthand understanding of the local challenges, combined with the ensuing deeper relationships, will mitigate many of the risks facing the change program. Firsthand experience will be invaluable when reviewing issues with the program timeline or budget with senior stakeholders. The reverse applies for the key staff working in the last 50 percent. They need to spend a month in the last 5 percent working environment to understand why managers from that market demand the level of "finish" that they do.

By way of simple example, a company operating in a first 5 percent market was engaged for a project in Saudi Arabia. Despite all the best practice followed when putting the budget and timeline together, they failed to realise that they would frequently encounter situations where the project team could not easily meet with many of the stakeholders as they worked in female-only rooms. When the original project plan was put together, the team evaluated the standard project risks, but did not consider that they would not have free access to the stakeholders. When the client reviewed the plan, they did not call out this restriction as it is such a normal part of their work environment it was not worth mentioning. The consequence was that both extra time and budget were required.

This is a simple example, but it does illustrate the value of in-country experience when establishing a new international business improvement project.

I close with the observation that international projects are generally led from last 5 percent countries. Investing time to build strong relationships founded on a proper understanding of each market, at the start of the change program, will build trust and mutual respect. Trust allows teams who are suffering the "tyranny of distance" that is common in international projects to raise issues earlier and more honestly. This, in turn, will more than compensate the additional costs invested at the start.

Printed in the United States
By Bookmasters